Christianity Explored

Rico Tice and Barry Cooper

Published by The Good Book Company
Elm House, 37 Elm Road, New Malden, Surrey KT3 3HB, UK
Telephone: 0845 225 0880; International: +44 (0) 208 942 0880
email: admin@thegoodbook.co.uk
UK: www.thegoodbook.co.uk
USA & Canada: www.thegoodbook.com
Australia: www.thegoodbook.com.au

ISBN: 9781904889342

Cover design by Carl Hamblin
Printed in the UK by CPI Bookmarque, Croydon

For Valerie Cooper
and Catherine Tice
who loved us unconditionally

Contents

Preface

You sometimes hear Christians talking about the Bible as if it were the last word on any subject. And I know that many of my readers will have a problem with that sort of attitude. Is it really possible for a sane person to reach the conclusion that the Bible is indeed God's way of speaking directly to human beings? On what grounds?

This is a simple illustration, but go with it. How do you know that a bag of sugar really contains sugar? Assuming you've been to the store and asked for a bag of sugar, how can you know that you've got what you paid for?

First of all, you could look at what it says on the bag. If it *claims* to be anything other than sugar, you might as well forget it. What does the Bible say about itself? It says it's 'God-breathed', that God speaks to us through it. Not that claiming something proves anything in itself. After all, I could *claim* to be two slices of apple pie. But any book that makes all the claims the Bible makes about itself demands some examination at least. For example, how many books insist that they hold the secret of eternal life, contain extraordinarily accurate prophecies (most of which have already come true, although some concern events yet to come), as well as claiming to show the only way that human beings can be saved from God's judgement? The Bible does all these things. Outrageous? It certainly seems to be. Provocative? Just a bit. True? It depends on who you ask. But even if there is only the tiniest, tiniest possibility that these claims might be true, the Bible deserves our attention. Because if the Bible did turn out to be the word of God, wouldn't it be extremely unwise to have deliberately ignored it?

Secondly, you could open up the bag to see what's inside. Does it *look* like sugar? And if we open the Bible and read it, it certainly *looks like* God's word. Approximately forty authors wrote in three different languages over a period of one thousand five hundred years. Some of the authors were young, some were old, some were soldiers, others were fishermen, farmers, civil servants or kings. They wrote during different periods of history, in different geographical locations, to different groups of people. It wasn't like a relay race, with one author handing on the baton to another. Often, they were writing centuries apart. But despite this amazing variation – which alone makes it a unique book – the Bible has one theme running through it like rings in the trunk of a tree. There is one striking message, one striking person at its centre. That person is the subject of *Christianity Explored*. Given the diversity of its origin, the long period of time over which the Bible was written, and the even longer period of history that it deals with, this single-minded purpose is quite staggering.

Then there are the fulfilled predictions that the Bible

contains – hundreds of them. There are more than 300 predictions that refer to Jesus Christ alone, 29 of which are fulfilled in the final 24 hours of his life. Despite the attacks of people who claim that the Bible is just like any other book, full of mistakes and contradictions, it may surprise you to learn that the Bible's authority was not seriously questioned for 15 centuries.

The book of Mark, which we'll be looking at in more detail, was written in about 65 AD. That's well within living memory of the events it records. So Mark knew that his first readers would easily be able to verify the truth of his account. But no one found fault. Even those who were hostile towards Jesus and his followers were unable to successfully dispute the historical accuracy of Mark's words. And even the harshest of today's critics have been unable to make any of their criticism stick. Furthermore, as you would expect from a book so grounded in historical realities, archaeological evidence has repeatedly confirmed the unwavering accuracy of biblical history. You see, it's important to remember that the Bible is not a collection of wisdom that may or may not be of interest to us. It is historical. For example, rather than just telling us that 'God is powerful', the Bible gives us real historical facts – such as the amazing deliverance of the Israelites from Egypt – that demonstrate the fact that God is powerful. So if you want to know whether or not there is any substance to the Bible, one way of doing it is to see if there is any substance to its historical claims.

Thirdly, you could always open the bag, dip your finger inside and actually taste it to see if it's sugar. That would really put the matter beyond doubt. You've heard people say that 'the proof of the pudding is in the eating', and the Bible is no exception to this rule. If you put the Bible into practice – and I hope that, by the end of this book, you'll want to – you'll see that the words the Bible contains could only have come from God. It *proves* itself to be God's word.

Don't be put off by those who tell you that the Bible can't be trusted. There are literally millions of people who would tell you otherwise. In any case, it's too important an issue to have other people form your opinion for you. Instead, I hope you'll want to see for yourself what the Bible says, examine its claims and then trust your own judgement.

Introduction

First of all, I have a confession to make. There is another book that has been around a lot longer than this one, and it has exactly the same aim: to make you familiar with who Jesus Christ was and why he is of absolute importance to everyone who has ever lived and ever will live. The person behind this other book is infinitely more gifted than I am, and the book's scope is admittedly superior to the one you're currently holding. Copies are readily available not only on the internet, in book stores and in libraries, but also in hotel rooms the world over, and it has been translated into more languages than any one person could reasonably be expected to master.

Actually, I'd better make that two confessions. The second is that I didn't have a particularly religious upbringing myself. In fact, my experience of Christianity was limited to a few dull sermons, slightly spooky people in strange garments hanging about in dank halls and religious education lessons during which I attempted to find references to rugby in the Bible. Christianity was worse than boring: it was a fiction. Jesus walking on water, the three wise men, the feeding of the five thousand, Father Christmas and Winnie the Pooh were all mixed up in my mind together. They were all make-believe, best left in the nursery.

So I was shocked when I discovered that my older

brother George had become a Christian. I remember telling him in no uncertain terms exactly what I thought about God and everything connected with God. To his credit, George didn't respond in kind. Instead, he pointed me to a single sentence in the Bible, the very first sentence of Mark chapter 1: 'The beginning of the gospel about Jesus Christ, the Son of God.' He explained that the word 'gospel' simply means 'good news'. 'Rico,' he said, 'you don't understand Christianity. You think it's all about church, men in dresses, obeying rules and beautiful old buildings, but it's not. It's just good news. Good news about Jesus Christ.'

Even my time in church, however, had brought me no closer to knowing what this 'good news about Jesus Christ' actually was. In fact, if I could hand the book you're now holding to the person I was twenty-odd years ago, that person would have dismissed it straight away. He wouldn't even have given it the benefit of the doubt, which is strange because – as I've since discovered – Jesus Christ is able to provide definitive answers to questions that were endlessly troubling to me. How can I be content? Is there any meaning to life? Is there life after death? Does God *really* exist or did we just make him up ourselves? If God exists, why is the world so full of injustice?

I suppose most of us already have an opinion about God. Some people look at the world, with all its suffering, and reject God out of hand. But other people have an inkling that yes, God probably does exist. They're not sure what He/She/It is like, but having seen the incredible scale and diversity of our universe, not to mention the beautiful form and function of our own minds and bodies, it seems like a reasonable proposition. The British astronomer Sir James Jeans certainly reached that conclusion. He wrote, 'The universe appears to have been designed by a pure mathematician.' For him, the amazing order of our universe – from the tiniest blood cell to the most distant galaxies – points to the existence of a master planner. Tom Stoppard, one of the most celebrated and intellectually rigorous playwrights of our time, wrote a play called *Jumpers*. When asked to talk about the play's theme, Stoppard said:

> A straight line of evolution from amino acid all the way through to Shakespeare's sonnets – that strikes me as possible, but a very long shot. Why back such an outsider? However preposterous the idea of God is, it seems to have an edge of plausibility.

'Atheism is a crutch for those who can't accept the reality of God', one of his characters says.

One other factor that has led some people to feel that God might exist is the human sense of loneliness, emptiness and restlessness, not to mention our sense of the infinite. That's why the background story of *The Matrix* is so ingenious: it feels like it *might* be true. In the film, Morpheus tells Neo:

> Let me tell you why you are here. It's because you know something. What you know you can't explain but you feel it. You've felt it your entire life. There is something wrong with the world. You don't know what it is, but it's there, like a splinter in your mind driving you mad.

(Come to think of it, that would be confession number three: I watch far too many films, as will become apparent.)

And it often seems as if nothing we do stops us feeling that way. A great job isn't enough. The car we've always wanted isn't enough. Friends aren't enough. Marriage and money aren't enough. Thom Yorke of the band Radiohead, in an interview with the *New Musical Express*, was asked about his ambitions:

> Ambitious for what? What for? I thought when I got to where I wanted to be everything would be different. I'd be somewhere else. I thought it'd be all white fluffy clouds. And then I got there. And I'm still here.

The interviewer asked him why he carried on making music, even though he'd already achieved the critical and commercial success he hoped for. 'It's filling the hole. That's all anyone does.' To the question, 'What happens to the hole?', Yorke paused a long time before answering: 'It's still there.' What Morpheus and Thom Yorke describe is nothing new. Augustine, writing in the fifth century, suggested a reason for this sense of 'wrongness' in our lives: 'O God, you have made us for yourself, and our hearts are restless till they find their rest in you.' Could he be right?

Having a vague sense that God might exist is one thing. According to recent polls, between 70 and 80 per cent of people in the UK have just that vague sense. But to believe that God actually *cares* intimately for those he has created probably seems a bit far-fetched to many. However, that is the claim the Bible makes. Furthermore, the Bible says, we can know God personally.

Imagine that you wanted to get to know the Queen personally. You could try writing a letter, or ringing her (don't bother looking in the directory), or you could try standing outside her gates with a very big sign. I don't recommend flying a light aircraft into her garden because the last person who tried that – funnily enough, an author trying to get some free publicity for his book – got arrested. The fact is, you wouldn't get very far with any of these approaches. Your only chance would be if she decided she wanted to meet you, came out of the palace, and introduced herself personally. And that is exactly what the Bible says God has done in Jesus Christ. It tells us that God wants to meet us, and that Jesus Christ is the one he's chosen to make the introduction.

Our choice

Now *if* the Bible's claim is true – that our creator wants to meet us through Jesus Christ – then that would affect all of us, whether we like it or not. Of course, we could choose to avoid investigating this claim. Alternatively, we could choose to examine the claim to see if it *is* true. But I am duty-bound to say that each of these choices will have serious implications for us.

A few years ago, a London newspaper conducted a revealing experiment. The *Evening Standard* had a person stand outside Oxford Circus underground station and offer people leaflets. On each was written a simple instruction: *Bring this piece of paper back to the person who gave it to you and they will give you £5. No strings attached.* People swarmed by, and lots actually took the leaflet, but in three hours only eleven came back. Apparently, most of us automatically assume that these bits of paper will be of no real interest, that they won't do us any good. (Actually, I'm sure I must have been one of those people who threw the leaflet away without even looking at it, and I've often kicked myself for being so stupid. Now, of course, I take every bit of paper I'm offered, so not only have I become extremely popular on Oxford Street, I've also become something of a fire hazard.)

My only plea is that you don't make that assumption. Don't assume that you've heard it all before and that reading the Bible will be of no use to you. Instead, I ask you simply to give it the benefit of the doubt as we focus on a single book of the Bible, a book named after its author, Mark. It's an accurate account of Jesus' life, written with the insight of those who spent years by Jesus' side. By making time to read Mark, you may begin to see – as I did – that Jesus Christ is the most conclusive proof anyone could have not only that God exists, but also that he made you, and that he cares passionately for you. In fact, Jesus answers all the difficult questions we posed a few paragraphs ago.

And if those kinds of answers frighten you, then, as they say before the football scores on the news, 'look away now...'

02

Who Was Jesus?

There's a great scene in the film *Notting Hill* in which the character Bernie meets Anna Scott, played by Julia Roberts, for the first time. Anna is a hugely famous Hollywood actress.

Bernie: So tell me, Anna, what do you do?

Anna: I'm an actress.

Bernie: I'm actually in the stock market myself, so not really similar fields, though I have done the odd bit of amateur stuff – P.G. Wodehouse farce, all that. I've always imagined that's a pretty tough job though, acting. I mean, the wages are a scandal, aren't they?

Anna: They can be.

Bernie: I see friends from university. They've been in the business longer than you. They're scraping by on £7–8,000 a year. It's no life. What sort of acting do you do?

Anna: Films mainly.

Bernie: Oh, splendid. Well done. How's the pay in movies? I mean, the last film you did, what did you get paid?

Anna: Fifteen million dollars.

Bernie: Right… so that's fairly good.

Bernie doesn't relate to Anna properly because he doesn't know who she is, and in order to relate to Jesus properly we have to get his identity right.

Was he a great moral teacher? A compassionate

miracle-worker? A misunderstood revolutionary? Mark's verdict goes far beyond any of these, as you can see from the very first sentence in his book:

The beginning of the gospel about Jesus Christ, the Son of God.

Noel Coward was once asked, 'What do you think about God?', to which he replied, 'We've never been properly introduced.' Well, that's exactly what Mark wants to do for us here. And he is determined that we see Jesus as a figure with divine authority: 'the Son of God'. Or, to put it another way, God in human form.

Now, to say such a thing seems outrageous to many modern ears, but it was no small matter to the people of Mark's day either. In fact, it got you thrown to the lions, because the only person you were supposed to treat with that kind of reverence was the Roman Emperor. Virgil, the Roman poet, described the emperors as a 'new breed of Man, come down from Heaven'. But here, right at the start of his book, Mark boldly tells us that no, there *is* a higher authority than the Emperor, and his name is Jesus. Mark then tries to justify this outrageous claim by providing evidence from Jesus' life.

Jesus has power and authority to teach
The first piece of evidence Mark gives concerning Jesus' true identity is in chapter 1 verses 21 and 22:

They [Jesus and some followers] went to Capernaum, and when the Sabbath came, Jesus went into the synagogue and began to teach. The people were amazed at his teaching, because he taught them as one who had authority, not as the teachers of the law.

One of the things that set Jesus apart from the religious leaders of the day (the 'teachers of the law') was the way he taught. The teachers of the law didn't come up with their own material. As with most of my sermons, the best stuff was taken from other people. There was nothing original in their teaching. They never taught without quoting the great teachers of the past, and they never claimed any authority of their own.

But Jesus did not teach like that. He didn't hide behind anybody else's authority – he claimed authority of his own. Rather than use the great teachers of the past to back up his arguments, he talks about himself. He says, 'I'm telling you this on my own authority – you can take it from me.' It's like someone in court who, rather than swearing on the Bible, simply says, 'I give you *my* word; there is no higher guarantee of truth.'

Jesus not only *claims* that his words have as much authority as God's words: when he speaks, it's as if somebody has suddenly switched on the lights in a dark room. His hearers are not merely impressed by his teaching, they are 'amazed'. What people in the synagogue heard from the lips of Jesus explained their lives to them. His teaching provided clear answers to the most difficult, obscure questions. And all this from a man who had no education to speak of.

We would, however, have every right to be even more wary of someone who claimed his teaching had the same authority as God's if his own life didn't match up to that teaching. At the age of 16, I started keeping a diary because I felt I owed it to the world to enshrine for posterity quite how great a bloke I was. What I found as I wrote in the diary was the contradiction between what I *said* about myself and what I actually *did*. I was surprisingly selfish, despite some good intentions, and I often ignored my words and ideals when it came to getting what I wanted. But Jesus was no hypocrite. His life was totally consistent with his teaching. He teaches, for example: 'Love your enemies and pray for those who persecute you.'[1] Later on, as he is suffering the most cruel and painful death imaginable, he prays, 'Father, forgive them, for they do not know what they are doing.'[2] Now *that* is practising what you preach.

So that's Mark's first point: Jesus has power and authority to teach.

Jesus has power and authority over sickness

But Jesus was no mere teacher. The second block of evidence Mark provides concerns Jesus' power and authority over sickness. One example of this is found in chapter 1 verses 29 to 31:

> As soon as they left the synagogue, they went with James and John to the home of Simon and Andrew. Simon's mother-in-law was in bed with a fever, and they told Jesus about her. So he went to her, took her hand and helped her up. The fever left her and she began to wait on them.

This is not an isolated incident. Three verses later, in verse 34, we read that Jesus cures whole crowds of sick people. A few days later, his touch cures a man who was suffering with a disease so serious that most people would have avoided any contact with the victim at all. But Jesus does reach out to touch him, and his simple touch is enough to cure his leprosy completely and immediately.

In fact, Jesus' power over sickness is such that even a *word* from his lips is enough to cure the most hopeless of

---

[1] Matthew chapter 5 verse 44   [2] Luke chapter 23 verse 34

cases. In the second chapter of Mark, for example, we read about a paralytic man who had to be lowered through a roof to meet Jesus – such was the density of the crowd that pressed to see him. He says to the paralytic, 'Get up, take your mat and go home' and, in full view of everyone, the man gets up and walks out, taking his mat with him. Not surprisingly, later in the chapter, everyone is saying, 'We have never seen anything like this!' The deaf hear, the blind see and the lame walk. Mark records 12 such examples of Jesus healing, and all of them show that Jesus' authority over sickness is far far greater than that of modern doctors – even with all of our admirable advances in medical technology.

Neither did these striking events go unnoticed by non-Christians of the time. Josephus, a Jewish historian writing in Section 18 of his book *Antiquities*, called Jesus 'a doer of wonderful deeds'. It's hard to disagree with that diagnosis.

Jesus has power and authority over nature
Mark shows that Jesus is an extraordinary teacher and healer, but in chapter 4 he goes even further.

Jesus and his followers (usually called 'disciples' in the Bible) are in a boat on the Lake of Galilee when a 'furious squall' comes up. Indeed, the word for 'furious squall' is actually closer to our word 'whirlwind'. It is a whirlwind so intense that waves break over their boat, which is practically sunk. And the disciples – some of whom are hardened fishermen – think they are going to die. They are totally at the mercy of the elements, and in their panic they wake Jesus, who is in the stern sleeping on a cushion: 'Teacher, don't you care if we drown?' And what does

Jesus do? Does he do a George Clooney, seize the helm and try heroically to wrestle the beleaguered boat out of the storm? No.

> He got up, rebuked the wind and said to the waves, 'Quiet! Be still!' Then the wind died down and it was completely calm.

It can take waves days to die down, but Jesus flattens them with a few words. At this stage, you could be forgiven for thinking, 'But that's impossible – human beings can't do that kind of thing.' And I'd agree with you. But that's exactly Mark's point: Jesus was not just another human being. Normal rules no longer apply. To be honest, I couldn't still my *bathwater* with a word, let alone a furious storm.

But that is exactly what this great teacher and healer does. And, in the light of this incident, is it enough to call Jesus 'a great teacher and healer'? For Mark, and for the startled disciples on that boat, it is not. They know that only God himself has control over the elements. So, looking at each other in terror, the disciples ask, 'Who is this? Even the wind and the waves obey him!' Whatever conclusion they – and we – draw, one thing is clear: Jesus has power and authority over nature. Furthermore, in the next chapter, these disciples witness something even more amazing. They see Jesus exert the same degree of control over death itself.

Jesus has power and authority over death

A lot of people share Woody Allen's sentiments on death: 'It's not that I'm afraid to die. I just don't want to be there when it happens.' The poet Philip Larkin lived most of his life tormented by the thought of death. For him, even life itself was 'slow dying'. But for some, especially the young, death seems a long way off. Another poet, Siegfried Sassoon, who lost many loved ones in World War I, wrote that 'at the age of twenty-two, I believed myself to be inextinguishable'.

There are many others who share that youthful bravado. I was certainly like that until the age of 16, when my godfather died after having lost his footing on a cliff path. Before that happened, I had no idea of the pain involved in death. And I'm not just talking about the pain felt by the person who is dying. There's the pain and despair felt by the family, the friends, all of whom feel the terrible sense of being separated from someone forever. Someone who loved and understood them. And those kinds of relationships are so hard to come by.

I recently picked up a bereavement card in a hospital shop, and on the inside it read: 'Those whom we have loved never really go away.' But that's a lie. That's the whole problem. The reason death is so fearful is because it has absolute power to separate us totally from those we love, often unexpectedly. And there's no comeback, no opportunity to tell them we love them one last time. There's nothing we can do to save them from it, however hard we wish. But, in the passage we'll look at now, Jesus confronts death *as its master*. Although *we* are powerless in the face of death, Jesus displays total authority over it.

In chapter 5 of Mark, there is a religious leader called Jairus. His little daughter is dying and – agonizingly – he is powerless to do anything about it. He falls at Jesus' feet and pleads with him to help, which is no small thing for a respected ruler at the local synagogue. He is desperate. So Jesus agrees to go with him to his house. As they are making their way there, something terrible happens.

> …some men came from the house of Jairus, the synagogue ruler. 'Your daughter is dead,' they said. 'Why bother the teacher any more?'

And, in that instant, the man's fragile hopes are shattered. They're too late. She's gone forever.

> Ignoring what they said, Jesus told the synagogue ruler, 'Don't be afraid; just believe.'

Now, it is a brave man who says something like that to a distraught father. A brave man – or at least one who is supremely confident of his own power.

> He did not let anyone follow him except Peter, James and John, the brother of James. When they came to the home of the synagogue ruler, Jesus saw a commotion, with people crying and wailing loudly. He went in and said to them, 'Why all this commotion and wailing? The child is not dead but asleep.' But they laughed at him.
>
> After he put them all out, he took the child's father and mother and the disciples who were with him, and went in where the child was. He took her by the hand and said to her, *'Talitha koum!'* (which means, 'Little girl, I say to you, get up!'). Immediately the girl stood up and walked around (she was twelve years old). At this they were completely astonished.

You can't get much more shocking than that. The man hears the terrible words, 'Your daughter is dead', but Jesus tells him not to worry, just to trust in his power over death. The child isn't dead, Jesus insists, she is merely sleeping. Thinking that he is speaking literally, the mourners laugh at him. They've seen the corpse. But Jesus takes the corpse's hand, tells her to get up, and she does so. The point is clear: for Jesus, it is as easy to raise somebody from the dead as it is for us to rouse somebody from sleep.

The challenge to us is this: having seen Jesus' authority over death, do we trust him enough to trust him with our own death? I was recently with a dying woman in a cancer hospice and because she, like Jairus, had placed her trust in Jesus, I was able to say to her with confidence: 'You are going to sleep and Christ will wake you from that sleep.' If we need more proof, we need look no further than Jesus' own death, and subsequent resurrection. We'll look at that in more detail in Chapter 6, but can I say at this point that if Jesus *does* have power over death, then it is madness to ignore him, to say 'I'm just not interested' or 'I don't have time' or 'That's nice, but it's not for me.' One day you and I will die. We may not fear it yet, but we can be absolutely certain of it. As Edward Norton's character says in the film *Fight Club*, 'On a long enough timeline, the survival rate for everyone drops to zero.' So Jesus' apparent power to overcome death is definitely worthy of our investigation.

Believe it or not, 'Quiet! Be still!' and 'Get up!' are not the most outrageous things Jesus says. For that, we're going to return to chapter 2 of Mark's Gospel, to the story of the paralytic man lowered through the roof by his friends.

Jesus has power and authority to forgive sins

Some men came, bringing to him a paralytic, carried by four of them. Since they could not get him to Jesus because of the crowd, they made an opening in the roof above Jesus and, after digging through it, lowered the mat the paralysed man was lying on. When Jesus saw their faith, he said to the paralytic, 'Son, your sins are forgiven.'

I can't imagine what the owner of the house thought as he saw his roof torn open. But what is particularly striking here is the first thing Jesus says to the paralysed man: 'Son, your sins are forgiven.' To the untrained eye, the man's most obvious problem would appear to be his inability to walk – so why not deal with that first? Why does Jesus home in on the problem of the man's 'sins'?

'Sin' is an old-fashioned word to many people. It has lost its meaning. When *The Independent* newspaper ran an article on the seven deadly sins, the writer had this to say: 'In this day and age, sin has lost its sting. A bit of sinning is much more likely to be seen as a spot of grown-up naughtiness; the kind of thing that sends a delicious shock through the system.' That's how most people think of sin – as a bit of fun on the side. But rightly understood, described as the Bible describes it, there is nothing nice about it. Jesus repeatedly insists that *sin is our biggest problem* – not paralysis, not global warming, not terrorism, not unemployment, not lack of love or education, but *sin*.

According to the Bible, sin is ignoring God in the world he has made. But why is ignoring God in this way so serious? Because it cuts us off from God. Because every time I insist on my independence in a world where God sustains everything, I am cutting myself off from the very source of all life. The Bible is clear that to live like that results in death – and not just death here, but eternal death.

As he talks to the paralysed man, Jesus makes the staggering claim that he has the authority to forgive this 'sin' which cuts us off from God: 'Son, your sins are forgiven.' The implications of this statement are not lost on the religious teachers who are sitting nearby. They don't mind the paralytic being called a sinner; they know from their Scriptures that everyone is a sinner. No, their problem with what Jesus says is more straightforward: 'He's blaspheming! Who can forgive sins but God alone?' They know that if we sin against God, only God can forgive us. (After all, if we do something wrong to another person, then only that person has the right to forgive us; it's nobody else's business.) By claiming to have forgiven the sins of the paralytic man, Jesus is putting himself in God's place. The religious teachers are deeply offended by this. But, as if to back up his claim, Jesus immediately heals the man with a few words. Jesus not only talks as if he is God, he also acts with God's power. So, once again, the question confronts us: just who is this man?

Mark's answer is clear. Jesus is 'the Son of God', 'the Lord' over sickness, nature, death and sin. Here, as he teaches, calms the storm, raises the dead, heals the sick and forgives sin, he is acting in God's world with God's authority. He behaves as if he is ruler over everything, as if he is God himself. And if that is true – that Jesus is God – then things start getting very personal for us as readers of Mark. Will I allow Jesus to be *my* Lord and teacher? Do I recognize that he has authority over *my* death, whether I like it or not? Can I see that he has the authority to forgive *my* sin, or to leave it unforgiven?

03

Jesus – His Aim

In 1991, when I went to college, I joined the local rugby club. Now the club was very competitive, so during the summer I received a long and strenuous training schedule in preparation for what was called 'Club Pre-Season Testing and Training' in September. I dutifully circled the date on my calendar, before throwing the schedule away and thinking, 'I'll go on some runs and do some sit-ups – I'll be fine.'

September rolled around eventually, after a fairly casual summer in which I nevertheless did more exercise than I had ever done before. In fact, I felt pretty confident as I turned up at the training ground. As I walked into the changing room, I noticed that all the blokes were very quiet. You spot this very quickly if it occurs in rugby players. Then the coach came in and said, 'Right, we'll start with the bleep test.' For the bleep test, we ran back and forth over a 20-yard stretch in time to a bleep that got faster and faster. We literally ran until we dropped. In my case, the 'drop' part was not long in coming.

Immediately after that, it was time for the fat tests. We had to strip down to our shorts which, as people who know me would tell you, is a terrifying thought. A machine with a large set of tweezers pinched the flesh on our biceps, triceps, stomachs, sides, thighs and calves. (There was one bloke who had an even higher percentage of body fat than I did. We became firm friends.) And so the tests went on. The results of each were recorded, and each test was – to a greater or lesser degree – humiliating. When it was finally over, the coach said, 'Well, it's not comfortable, but at least we've found out the truth here on the training ground before the real questions get asked out there on the playing field. Some of you have really been exposed, haven't you?'

Listening to what Jesus has to say about you and me is like going through fitness tests. It means being told what we are really like beneath the surface, and it is a very uncomfortable experience. In a way, a better title for this chapter would be 'I wish I didn't have to tell you this, but…'

The last chapter described Jesus' unique power and authority to teach, cure illness, calm storms and raise the dead. In the light of that, we might ask, 'Why? What was Jesus' ultimate aim in doing these things?' Did he want to bring peace on earth? (That's the Jesus of Christmas cards.) Did he want to end the sufferings of the world? (That's Jesus the great healer.) Did he want to give us a supreme example of how we should live and treat each other? (That's Jesus as a sort of schoolteacher.) Or was he aiming to bring about the reform of society? (That's Jesus the political activist.) Although there is an element of truth in all of those possibilities, Mark's Gospel doesn't give any of them as Jesus' ultimate aim.

Jesus came to rescue rebels

Mark wants us to know that the reason Jesus came was to rescue 'sinners': those who have rebelled against God. Look at chapter 2 verses 14 to 17:

> As he [Jesus] walked along, he saw Levi son of Alphaeus sitting at the tax collector's booth. 'Follow me,' Jesus told him, and Levi got up and followed him.
>
> While Jesus was having dinner at Levi's house, many tax collectors and 'sinners' were eating with him and his disciples, for there were many who followed him. When the teachers of the law who were Pharisees saw him eating with the 'sinners' and tax collectors, they asked his disciples: 'Why does he eat with tax collectors and "sinners"?'
>
> On hearing this, Jesus said to them, 'It is not the healthy who need a doctor, but the sick. I have not come to call the righteous, but sinners.'

In this passage there are two groups of people: the goodies and the baddies. The baddies are made up of people such as Levi, who is a tax collector. Bear in mind that tax collectors were even less popular then than they are now. In fact, they were universally reviled as traitors, working as they did for the occupying Roman forces.

The goodies in this passage are the senior religious figures of the day, the Pharisees. They are the religious establishment, their credentials as religious people are hugely impressive, they seem whiter than white. The question is: who would you expect Jesus to hang around with? The tax collector, or the local church leader? Instinctively we'd expect him to want to be with the goodies, the religious people, the elite. It would be a bit like a school prize-giving, with Jesus patting the religious do-gooders on the back, while scum like Levi look on enviously. But this is the shock for us (as indeed it was for them): 'It is not the healthy who need a doctor, but the sick. I have not come to call the righteous, but sinners.'

It upsets the religious people enormously to hear this powerful and authoritative figure say, 'I can heal you, but if you don't think you need a cure, you can forget it. I'm here for the sick.' Jesus makes it clear that people who think they are good enough without him don't want his help, just as healthy people don't want doctors. That's a problem for a lot of us. As Tom Ripley says in *The Talented Mr Ripley*: 'Whatever you do, however terrible, however hurtful, it all makes sense, doesn't it, in your head? You never meet anybody that thinks they're a bad person.' But Jesus says here, 'I've come for people who *realize* that they're bad people, for those who know that they're living as rebels in God's world.' In other words, for sinners.

So, the qualification for coming to Jesus is not 'Are you good enough?' but 'Are you bad enough?' Jesus is categorically not interested in people who think they are good. He is devoted to those who realize that they are bad. Jesus' aim is to call rebels back into a relationship with the God who made them, with the God who gives them each breath and yet is treated like a footnote in their lives. In the next chapter we'll see exactly how Jesus achieves that rescue, but for now I want to focus on the assumption Jesus makes: that we are *all* rebels in need of rescue, even if we believe we're basically good people.

We are all rebels

Did you detect a note of sarcasm when Jesus refers to the Pharisees as 'righteous' ('I have not come to call the righteous, but sinners')? Jesus recognizes that although the Pharisees are righteous by their own standards, they are not righteous by God's standards. If we are in any doubt about this, fast forward to Mark chapter 3 where these Pharisees, these people who consider themselves good enough for God, begin jealously plotting to kill Jesus. Clearly, despite what they may think, the Pharisees need rescuing just as much as anyone else does. Jesus makes it quite clear that *everyone* – however 'good' they consider themselves to be – is in desperate need of rescue.

If that idea grates with you, as it certainly once did with me, then we need to expose ourselves to a tough question: what is the world *really* like? If we take an honest look at the world, we will see good and evil mixed together. We take a stroll in the park and see a little child toddle excitedly towards its mother with arms outstretched. Nearby is a young couple ambling slowly along, lost in each other's company. When we see those kinds of things we think – quite rightly – that this world is a pretty special place. As Rickie Fitts says in *American Beauty*, 'Sometimes there's so much beauty in the world I feel like I can't take it, like my heart's going to cave in.' But then, if the child in the park falls over and starts screaming, we remember that pain is never far behind happiness in our world. If the loving couple starts shouting angrily at one another, we recall the article in the newspaper saying that nearly one in two marriages end in divorce. The world is not all bad, but who can honestly claim that it's all good? At least one hundred *million* people died violent deaths during the one hundred years of the twentieth century. That's more than during the previous 19 centuries *put together*. It seems safe to say that war and death are as much a part of our world as peace and life. And there are certainly no signs of improvement. If anything, the reverse is true.

Yes, Louis Armstrong was right to say that it's a wonderful world, but we have to admit that there is something profoundly wrong with it, too. We sense that the world could be, *should* be, a wonderful place – but the reality repeatedly dashes our hopes. The Bible says that we have our sense of what *should* be because God made you and me 'in his image'. In other words, because we are like him in lots of ways, we also have his sense of perfection. The Bible goes on to say that the reason the *world* is not as it should be is because *we* are not as we should be. That, says Jesus, is why we need rescuing.

And yet it still offends us to think that we need anyone's help. Of course, some people are definitely 'bad' – murderers and rapists for a start – but not *us*, and certainly not our family and our friends. We're basically good people with a few human faults here and there. We tend to be confident that our good points outweigh the bad, that we are good enough for God. But at this point we need to ask another tough question: what are we *really* like? The truth is that we're much more flawed than we're willing to admit.

I came across this gleeful advertisement recently on the internet:

> You're in Serious Trouble – It's a Proven Fact! Deleting 'Internet Cache and History' will NOT protect you, because any of the web pages, pictures, movies, videos, sounds, e-mail, chat logs and everything else you see or do could easily be recovered to haunt you forever! How would you feel if a snoop made this information public to your spouse, mother and father, neighbours, children, boss or the media? It could easily ruin your life!

The people who wrote that certainly understood that human beings are susceptible to great weakness on occasion. I understood this fact for myself when my brother once challenged me to think, say and do nothing impure, unkind or untrue for 15 minutes (I don't think I made it past the first minute). And it's not only the things we've said, done and thought that are a problem. There are the things we *didn't* say, do and think. People we should have helped, perhaps. Those lapses which may have bothered our consciences at the time but which were forgotten an hour or two later. Or there may be other, more bitter failures that we have never been able to forget. If all my thoughts, words and actions were displayed for all my friends and family to see, it would be a nightmare. I wouldn't even be able to make eye contact with them, I would be so ashamed.

So what's the problem? Why is there so much to be ashamed of? Verses 18 to 23 of Mark chapter 7 have the answer. The Pharisees have been arguing that it's the *external* things that make us 'bad': the things we touch, the places we go, the things we eat. But Jesus tells his disciples that the problem is much closer to home:

> 'Are you so dull?' he asked. 'Don't you see that nothing that enters a man from the outside can make him "unclean"? For it doesn't go into his heart but into his stomach, and then out of his body.'... He went on: 'What comes out of a man is what makes him "unclean." For from within, out of men's hearts, come evil thoughts, sexual immorality, theft, murder, adultery, greed, malice, deceit, lewdness, envy, slander, arrogance and folly. All these evils come from inside and make a man "unclean".'[1]

---

[1] For the sake of clarity, I should point out that the word 'man' here refers to all mankind (in other words, all human beings).

The problem, says Jesus, is our hearts. *They* make us unclean. If we were to trace all the evil in the world back to its source, the place we'd end up is the human heart. To the people of Jesus' day, the heart wasn't just the pump that sent blood around our veins. It wasn't even simply the emotional core of the body. It was even more than that: it was 'the real you', the inner you, the seat of human personality. Why is it so hard to keep good relationships going? Why do we hurt even those we love most? Why aren't people at work more co-operative? Because each of us has a heart problem.

Unfortunately, according to Jesus, our problems don't end there. It's not just the fact that we often treat each other in a shameful way: *we treat God in that way too.* (And just as there are consequences when we treat other human beings carelessly, so there are consequences when we neglect God.) Look at Mark chapter 12 verses 28 to 31, where Jesus is debating with some religious leaders:

> One of the teachers of the law came and heard them debating. Noticing that Jesus had given them a good answer, he asked him, 'Of all the commandments, which is the most important?'

This was a famously tricky question to answer. *Which of God's commands is the most important?* All the religious leaders debated it endlessly. After all, God made us and sustains us. He gives us every good thing we enjoy. Not only that, he has power and authority over our lives. So how should we respond to him? Jesus answers quickly and clearly: 'Love the Lord your God with all your heart and with all your soul and with all your mind and with all your strength.'

Note the word 'all': no part of our life is to be cordoned off from God. The appropriate response to a God who is deeply and personally committed to us is that he deserves all of everything we are. But, in reality, God has had all of nothing. *We* decide exactly what we'll do with our hearts, minds, souls and strength. We give our hearts to many things, but we keep them from our God. We barely know his commands, let alone seek to obey them.

I read Anthea Turner's autobiography, *Fools Rush In* (for research purposes, in case you're wondering), and in it she talks about her difficult and well-publicized relationships. At one point she describes the time she went to a Whitney Houston concert: 'Whitney had real star quality and I was hugely impressed. When she sang the lines, "learning to love yourself is the greatest love of all", I nearly cried. She was spot on.' But is loving ourselves really the greatest love of all? What does it achieve for us? The tragic fact is that in doing so, we turn our backs on the very relationship for which we were primarily designed, because we were designed first and foremost to love *God*. Instead, we live as if we *were* God, ignoring our loving creator who gives us all that we cherish: love, friends, laughter – even life itself. We decide what is right and wrong, we are our only point of reference, and we are the highest authority. We ignore the very person who is keeping us alive.

And that fact brings us to the final point.

We are in danger
The passengers on the *Titanic* didn't know that they were heading for trouble. As they headed for the iceberg, they

were having the party of their lives. In the film, there were even those who deliberately ignored the warnings. But whether they liked it or not, the reality was that every single person on that ship was in serious danger.

Let's look now at the harshest verses of Mark's Gospel in order to determine the reality of our own situation. In these verses – Mark chapter 9 verses 43 to 48 – Jesus himself warns us just how serious our sin really is:

> 'If your hand causes you to sin, cut it off. It is better for you to enter life maimed than with two hands to go into hell, where the fire never goes out. And if your foot causes you to sin, cut it off. It is better for you to enter life crippled than to have two feet and be thrown into hell. And if your eye causes you to sin, pluck it out. It is better for you to enter the kingdom of God with one eye than to have two eyes and be thrown into hell...'

Because of our sin, we are in terrible danger and, if we ignore Jesus' warning, we will be punished by God. The Bible says that hell is the place where, for all eternity, people will be punished if they die still rebelling against their creator. It will be a real place of conscious pain. Believe me, I take no pleasure in relating these words of Christ, just as God takes no pleasure in punishing people. The reason God warns us about hell is because he loves us and does not want us to go there.

When I was in Australia staying with a friend, he took me to a beach on Botany Bay. It was deserted, the sun was out, and the clear water was completely calm. I decided I had to go for a swim, but just as I was taking off my shirt, my friend said in a broad Aussie accent, 'Mate, what are you doing?' I told him I was going for a dip. 'But what about these signs?', he said, pointing to a huge billboard behind me. It read: 'Danger – Sharks. No Swimming.' It seemed hard to believe, because everything looked so calm and beautiful. He must have seen my incredulous reaction, because he continued very dryly, 'Listen, mate, 200 Australians have been killed by sharks over the years. And you have to work out whether those signs are there to save you, or to ruin your fun. You're of age, you decide.' With that he walked off up the beach, and I rather sheepishly put my shirt back on.

The words of Jesus are like a huge warning sign to us. They have been written down in order to try and protect us. But many people – understandably – want to dismiss this disturbing idea of hell as a fairy tale. They don't see how serious their sin is. Like the passengers on the *Titanic*, they are blind to the fact that they need to be rescued. But ask yourself this question: if hell is not a reality, why did Jesus bother coming at all? 'I have not come to call the righteous, but sinners.' If sinners don't really need rescuing, why the rescue mission?

According to Jesus, hell is real. So much so that we should do anything to avoid it. 'If your hand causes you to sin, cut it off. It is better for you to enter life maimed than with two hands to go into hell.' If the problem is the foot, we should cut it off. If the problem is the eye, we should gouge it out. But here is the crux of our predicament: where is the root of all our problems, according to Jesus? *The heart*. If it was the eye, or the foot, or the hand, we could sort that out, but we can't cut out our heart.

And that is why we need Jesus to rescue us. 'It is not the healthy who need a doctor, but the sick...' As much as I hated the fat tests and the bleep tests, I would still rather be exposed as unfit on the training ground than in front of spectators in a key match. That's exactly what Jesus does, exposing what we are really like so that we can do something about it while there is still time. If there's no danger, we can forget about Jesus, put down this book, and get on with our lives. But if there is any possibility that we might face punishment from God, then ignoring Jesus would be as foolish as swimming with the sharks.

04

Jesus – His Death

I recently picked up a biography of Winston Churchill and searched the index. Even though it was a fairly weighty book with about three hundred pages, only three pages were devoted to the subject of his death. In the Gospels (the books of Matthew, Mark, Luke and John in the Bible), about *one third* of each Gospel is given over to Jesus' death. We've seen how amazing his life was – so why spend so much time dwelling on his death?

Indeed, why is it that his mode of death – the cross – has become a universally-recognized symbol of Christianity? Christians might have chosen a manger to remind them of Jesus' birth, or an empty tomb to remind them of his resurrection. Perhaps a scroll to remind them of his teaching or a lamp to signify a brilliant life lived in an otherwise dark world. But no, they chose a cross – a reminder of his death. No other religion celebrates the death of its founder.

Not only that, but Christians celebrate the cross – a particularly horrendous Roman method of execution reserved for common criminals. The Roman orator Cicero described it like this:

> But the executioner, the veil that covers the condemned man's head, the cross of crucifixion, these are horrors which ought to be far removed not only from the person of a Roman citizen

> but even from his thoughts and his gaze and his hearing. It is
> utterly wrong that a Roman citizen, a free man, would ever be
> compelled to endure or tolerate such dreadful things.[1]

The cross was deliberately made cruel and gruesome so that any slave considering rebellion would pass by the crucified victim and think to himself, 'However terrible my life is, rebellion is not worth it.' Small wonder that the late comedian Bill Hicks observed: 'A lot of Christians wear crosses around their necks. Do you think when Jesus comes back he's going to want to look at a cross?' But Christians aren't ashamed of the cross. In fact, they seem *proud* of it. Paul, another writer in the Bible, says this: 'May I never boast except in the cross of our Lord Jesus Christ'.[2]

Why should this be? Take a look at Mark chapter 8 verse 31:

> He [Jesus] then began to teach them that the Son of Man
> [meaning himself] must suffer many things and be rejected
> by the elders, chief priests and teachers of the law, and that he
> must be killed and after three days rise again.

Notice the word 'must'. Jesus is saying not only that he will die, but that his death is *necessary* in some way. Similarly, look at Jesus' words in Mark chapter 10 verse 45:

> 'For even the Son of Man did not come to be served, but to
> serve, and to give his life as a ransom for many.'

The 'Faith Zone' in the Millennium Dome (remember that?) said that Jesus was a good man who died tragically

---

[1] Michael Grant, *Cicero, Murder Trials* (Middlesex: Penguin, 1975). [2] Galatians chapter 6 verse 14

young. But that misses the point. Jesus died in order to pay 'a ransom for many'. He died to rescue rebels by paying the price to free them. Suddenly, the thought of *celebrating* the cross seems less strange. Because although the danger we are in is very real, the cross is our lifeboat. It is how Jesus rescues people.

And to understand this fully, we need to read Mark's account of the crucifixion in chapter 15, which tells us three things about the cross: *God was angry, Jesus was abandoned* and *we can be accepted*.

1. God was angry

To God-fearing Jews of the time, darkness in the daytime was a sign of God's anger. Time and again in the Bible, light represents God's presence and favour, while darkness tells us that God is acting in judgement. For example, God judged Pharaoh by sending darkness over the land when he refused to release the Jews from slavery in Egypt. Now, in Mark chapter 15 verse 33, we read about this startling incident that occurs while Jesus is on the cross:

> At the sixth hour [12 noon] darkness came over the whole land until the ninth hour [3 p.m.].

Mark counts the hours according to the Jewish system of timekeeping, and he tells us that just when the sun should be burning brightest, at midday, darkness suddenly falls. A bit like a solar eclipse, except that this couldn't have been a solar eclipse. Why not? The crucifixion happened during the Jewish festival of Passover, which always fell on a full moon, but the moon cannot be full if it is positioned between the sun and the earth for an eclipse. In addition to that, solar eclipses never last more than six minutes. This darkness lasted *three hours*. Something supernatural is occurring, and the clear message is that God is angry.

Sometimes people think of anger as something irrational, unpredictable and wild. But God's anger is different. It is his controlled, personal hostility towards all that is wrong.

A God who is good is right to be angry about sin. He doesn't lean back in a rocking chair, light up his pipe, and pretend nothing has happened. No, sin matters to God. So lying matters to God, as does selfishness. Likewise, adultery matters to him. Greed matters to him. Murder matters. The deaths of Kosovan women and children because they are from the wrong ethnic group matter to God, as do the deaths of those in the World Trade Center, and he will not simply overlook them. If those things matter to us, then they certainly matter to the God who made us and gave us loving laws to live by. The difference is that when *I* get angry about these things, I'm powerless to do anything about it. And, often, so is our justice system. It's not possible to give back the murdered daughter to her distraught parents, or restore the innocence of a child who has been abused. We might think to ourselves, *'If God existed, he'd do something about all this.'* Well, he *has* done something about injustice. He did it on the cross.

As Jesus was dying on the cross, the darkness that came over the whole land tells us that *God was acting in anger to punish sin*. But that leaves us with a question: whose sin was God angry at? The staggering answer is that God seems to be angry at Jesus.

2. Jesus was abandoned

There is no doubt that Jesus suffered great physical agony on the cross, but the information Mark relays here in chapter 15 verse 34 speaks of *spiritual* agony:

> And at the ninth hour Jesus cried out in a loud voice, *'Eloi, Eloi, lama sabachthani?'* – which means, 'My God, my God, why have you forsaken me?'

On the cross, Jesus was abandoned by God and experienced what it means to be cut off from God, his loving Father, for the first time in all eternity. 'My God, my God, why have you forsaken me?' Previously, Jesus had addressed God as 'Father', or 'Abba', a word even more intimate than 'Daddy'. But not here. He is experiencing a horrific and terrible separation that he has never known. God is doing something he only ever does by way of punishment.

But Jesus had never rebelled against God. According to those who knew him, Jesus lived a sinless life. He had done nothing that deserved punishment. So why was he being punished? The answer is that he was being punished for *our* sin.

Imagine a video that captures every detail of your life. It reveals far more than we saw in *The Truman Show* or *Big Brother,* because it manages to record your thoughts and your motives, as well as your actions and words. It's a record that covers your whole life, all the way from birth to death. As you watch it, there are lots of moments to cherish and of which you can feel proud. There are loving relationships, wonderful achievements, genuine honesty. You see plenty of things that are worthy of applause and approval, things that make you want to hit the rewind button so that you can watch them again and again. In these moments you see God's gifts being well used. But, of course, there are also many moments of which you rightly feel ashamed, moments that make you want to hit fast forward. Selfish actions, unkind thoughts, words you've only spoken because you knew you wouldn't be heard. All of it is recorded faithfully on the video. The question is: would we want this video played in front of people we know? Sir Arthur Conan Doyle, creator of Sherlock Holmes, sent a telegram as a joke one night to the 12 most respected people he could think of. It read: 'Flee! All is revealed!' Within 24 hours, six of those people had left the country in a panic. Like them, we all have secrets that we would hate to have exposed. The Bible's way of describing the video is 'the unfavourable record of our debts'.[3] And this record of our debts (or 'sin') separates us from God. In fact, the Bible says that God is so pure that even one frame from that video would be enough to separate us from him.

When we ignore God, doing things 'our way', treating him as if he's not really important at all, it's no cause for celebration. Because when we do that, it breaks our relationship with him. We have no cause to feel proud of those times when we've treated him as if he were a servant, then blamed him when things have not gone as we wanted them to. Can you imagine treating a friend like that? Would you expect that relationship to last long?

As we've seen, this treatment of God ultimately results in God allowing us to make that choice. He is a just judge, and in the end, if we insist upon living apart from him, he will give us what we insist upon. If we continue saying to

---

[3] Colossians chapter 2 verse 14 (GNB)

him, 'Leave me alone', then there will come a day when with great sadness God will say, 'OK. I'll leave you alone. I'll let you have what you want.' This is what the Bible calls hell: to be without God, and all that that entails. It means being without the love of others. It is to be utterly alone, with no hope or comfort.

And that is why Jesus cried out, 'My God, my God, why have you forsaken me?' as he hung on the cross. He was experiencing God's punishment. And it couldn't have been *his* sin that made him feel separated from God, because the Bible tells us that Jesus was free from sin. No, it was *our* sin that separated him from God. In those agonizing moments, Jesus was taking upon himself all the punishment that our sin, everything on that video, deserves. The Bible tells us again and again that our rebellion against God deserves punishment, and punishment is exactly what Jesus endured *on our behalf*. As Jesus died on the cross, he willingly died for me, as my substitute, in my place, taking the punishment I deserve.

The result of this extraordinary self-sacrifice is simply this: *Jesus paid the price for sin so that we never have to.* The amazing truth is that Jesus loved me enough to die for me – for me, and for all the people who put their trust in him.

3. We can be accepted

What Mark does in verses 37 and 38 is strange. He records the moment of Jesus' death, but then turns his attention to something that happens simultaneously at the temple, which is on the other side of the city. He wants us to understand that the two events are connected in some way:

> With a loud cry, Jesus breathed his last.
> The curtain of the temple was torn in two from top to bottom.

As soon as Jesus dies, we're transported to the interior of Jerusalem's huge temple. We see an incredible thing. The temple curtain is 30 feet high and as thick as the span of a man's hand. It is made from a single piece of material. Suddenly we hear a thunderous ripping sound and the curtain falls to the ground in two pieces.

But we'll only understand why that matters when we realize what the curtain stood for. On 11 November 1989, the Berlin Wall was broken down, showing that the Cold War between East and West had ended. In the same way, when the curtain in the temple was ripped in two, the Cold War between God and us was ended. The curtain was actually a terrifying barrier to the 'Holy of Holies', the heart of the temple where God was said to live. So holy was this place that only the High Priest could enter it once a year. Not just any person, and not even any priest, but only the High Priest, once he had performed an elaborate series of sacrifices, and then only once a year. The whole system was designed to show that it was not an easy thing to come into the presence of God. This thick, towering curtain was like a huge 'No Entry' sign. It very clearly said that it is impossible for sinful people like you and me to walk into God's presence. Then suddenly, as Jesus dies, this curtain is ripped in two by God, from top to bottom. God is saying that the way is now open for us to enter his presence. The barriers are now down, and there is nothing to prevent us from enjoying a relationship with him. How is this made possible? Because Jesus was willing to be abandoned. He has taken God's anger on our behalf so that we can be accepted.

I once read a story about a man caught in a forest fire. He'd had a remarkable escape and was asked how he'd managed to survive. Apparently, as he saw the fire being swept toward him by the wind, he realized that the flames were moving too fast to run away from. Instead, he took some matches from his pocket and started setting fire to the area immediately downwind of him. Soon he had formed a patch of burned grass. He then stood in the middle of the burned patch and, although the fire overtook him, it could not burn the grass immediately around him because he had already burned it. The man knew that fire cannot burn the same patch of grass twice. This little story illustrates a truth that the Bible teaches: as God's anger burns against the sin that Jesus took upon himself at the cross, it burns once and for all. Once the judgement falls, it cannot fall again. We can be accepted by God because the punishment we deserve has fallen – once and for all – on Jesus:

> He was despised and rejected by men,
> a man of sorrows, and familiar with suffering.
> Like one from whom men hide their faces
> he was despised, and we esteemed him not.
> Surely he took up our infirmities
> and carried our sorrows,
> yet we considered him stricken by God,
> smitten by him, and afflicted.
> But he was pierced for our transgressions,
> he was crushed for our iniquities;

the punishment that brought us peace was upon him,
and by his wounds we are healed.
We all, like sheep, have gone astray,
each of us has turned to his own way;
and the LORD has laid on him the iniquity of us all.

It's a remarkable poem. Firstly, because it tells us that although 'each of us has turned to his own way', God nevertheless wants to rescue us. And second, because this description of what happened at the cross was written about seven hundred years before it actually happened. You can find the rest of the poem in Isaiah chapter 53.

So, how should we respond to the cross? Mark's account of the crucifixion focuses not only on Jesus, but also on the reactions of those who witness the event. It is as if Mark is saying, 'This is how others responded to what happened at the cross. How will you respond?' There are a number of different reactions recorded in Mark chapter 15.

Reaction 1: The busy soldiers

When we first meet them, they are mocking Jesus – in particular his claim to be King of the Jews. The whole company spit on him and beat him, before leading him to the place of execution.

They brought Jesus to the place called Golgotha (which means The Place of the Skull). Then they offered him wine mixed with myrrh, but he did not take it. And they crucified him.

There's a glimmer of compassion here because they know what Jesus is about to suffer. They offer him wine mixed with myrrh, a bitter drug to help dull the agony, but he will not take it. They then crucify him. And what is their response to this agonizing spectacle?

Dividing up his clothes, they cast lots to see what each would get.

For the soldiers, the greatest legacy of the cross will be the garments left by the dead man. They're absorbed in simply doing their job. And as they do so, they notice nothing special about him. Here's a frightening thought: as they are 'just doing their job', they are missing the significance of the most important death in history. They are blind to it. No doubt they are doing their job well, but in doing their duty they miss the true legacy of the cross. And there are millions of people today who are like these soldiers. They're occupied with work, with doing their duty, with paying their mortgage. The daily activities of their intense lives keep them from seeing the significance of the cross.

Reaction 2: The self-satisfied religious

The religious leaders are already convinced that they know the way to God, so Jesus Christ is irrelevant to them. And – as far as they're concerned – the cross proves it:

…the chief priests and the teachers of the law mocked him among themselves. 'He saved others,' they said, 'but he can't save himself!'

They're convinced that they have their own means of gaining access to God, and it certainly doesn't involve anything as shameful and pathetic as the cross. Mark implies that often it is precisely these types of people – those who have created their own man-made religion, or who follow their own morality – who are the most vicious opponents of the cross. Despite their 'spiritual' appearance, they do not want to be accepted by God in this way. They can't bear to admit that they cannot help themselves. The cross is offensive to them, as it was to George Bernard Shaw, who stood up at a Christian meeting during which the cross was being explained and shouted, 'I will pay for my sin myself!' Again, they are blind to the seriousness of sin, and therefore blind to the true significance of Jesus' death.

Reaction 3: Pilate, the coward

Pontius Pilate is the Roman governor of the area. The sign he has had put up over Jesus' head appears sympathetic. It reads: 'The King of the Jews'. All the Gospel writers assure us that Pilate is convinced of Jesus' innocence. He tries again and again to free Jesus from the clutches of the religious authorities who are exerting tremendous pressure on Pilate to have Jesus killed. But, eventually, he hands Jesus over to be crucified. He knows deep down in his heart that Jesus doesn't deserve to be crucified, and so he utters those chilling words recorded by Matthew, another Gospel writer: 'I am innocent of this man's blood. It's your responsibility.'

Why, then, does he hand over an innocent man to be executed? The answer lies in Mark chapter 15 verse 15: 'Wanting to satisfy the crowd, Pilate released Barabbas to them. He had Jesus flogged, and handed him over to be crucified.' Pilate is a crowd-pleaser. Like many people, he is unwilling to stand out from the crowd, and he is subject to considerable pressure from those around him. His nerve cracks and he gives in to the desires of others, even though he knows Jesus is innocent. When it really matters, when the world is against him, he won't stand up for Jesus. Pilate was a coward who abandoned an innocent man. And although he didn't realize it at the time, Pilate abandoned someone who was a great deal more than that.

Reaction 4: The bystander who came for the show

Mark then records the reaction of an individual in the crowd. The man wishes to see if Elijah will come and rescue Jesus. (In Jewish legend, Elijah was celebrated as one who helped those in need.) The man has a sort of superstitious fascination as he contemplates the cross. He offers Jesus a sponge filled with wine vinegar, presumably to help postpone an inevitable death, but nothing in the scene moves him to awe, reverence, or even pity. He just wants to experiment while Jesus dies. He is totally detached from what is happening.

Just before he died, the writer Kingsley Amis said this in an interview with the *Daily Telegraph*:

> One of Christianity's great advantages is that it offers an explanation for sin. I haven't got one. Christianity's got one enormous thing right – original sin – for one of the great benefits of organised religion is that you can be forgiven your sins, which must be a wonderful thing.

The interviewer records that here Amis bowed his head and said, 'I mean, I carry my sins around with me. There's nobody to forgive them.' Although he admits his need for forgiveness, he remains detached from the forgiveness that the cross provides. For whatever reason, Kingsley Amis remained a spectator while Jesus Christ was offering him the one thing he craved most. The curtain has been torn from top to bottom, the way is open to God, but the spectator walks away from the cross untouched.

Some people think it's fine to be a bystander. They think that they don't need to do anything in the light of Jesus' death, that even spectators automatically receive the benefit. But the truth is that I only benefit from the death of Jesus if I put my trust in it.

Mark is telling us that no one can remain neutral when they consider the cross. We are either too busy like the soldiers, too self-satisfied like the religious, too cowardly like Pilate, or too detached like the bystander.

Actually, there *is* one last possible reaction to the cross. This response, made by the Roman centurion, is the culmination of everything we've read so far.

Reaction 5: The Roman centurion

He is a hard-bitten Roman soldier, the equivalent of a Regimental Sergeant Major, a veteran in charge of a hundred men. He has doubtless fought many gruelling campaigns and seen many men die, but he has never seen a man die like this. And as he watches Jesus on the cross, he realizes something:

> ...when the centurion, who stood there in front of Jesus, heard his cry and saw how he died, he said, 'Surely this man was the Son of God!'

Despite being one of those responsible for carrying out the execution, the centurion acknowledges Jesus to be the Son of God. His words echo and affirm those words we remember from the very beginning of Mark's Gospel – 'the gospel about Jesus Christ, the Son of God'. And that is our final possibility as we look at what happened at the cross. We can recognize that Jesus is telling the truth. That he is indeed the Son of God.

Looking across London's skyline, you can see the home of British justice, the Old Bailey. On top of the building is Pomeroy's magnificent golden statue of the goddess Justicia. In one hand she is holding the scales of justice and in the other she holds the sword of wrath. The fact that she is blindfolded is a warning to us: no matter who we are, if we are found to be guilty, the sword of wrath *must* fall. If you then let your gaze wander across the skyline a short distance you'll find another golden object, this time topping St Paul's cathedral. It's a cross, and it is a powerful reminder that although the sword of wrath must fall, it fell on Jesus Christ. In that moment our indignant cries for justice were perfectly satisfied and, in that same moment, our desperate calls for God's mercy were lovingly answered. And, in the light of that, what should I do with my sin? Will I take it to the cross to be forgiven, or will I take it with me to my grave, and to the judgement that must fall?

05

What Does 'Grace' Mean?

I was once at a dinner party in Dorset, sitting next to a school friend's wife. She told me, 'The most important thing about religion, Rico, is that it's there when you need it.' So I asked her how she would feel if her husband treated her like that. An almost imperceptible pause. 'Well, he wouldn't.' 'Yes, but just supposing he did?' This time through gritted teeth: 'If he treated me like that I'd murder him.' Which begged the question, 'Well how do you think God feels about you using him only when you need him?' To which she replied (as if she was bored with the whole subject), 'Look, I'm sorry, but that is just not the way I see religion. Religion to me is that God is there for me in the rough times.'

Now, I'm going to ask you to scribble down your answer to a question which cuts right to the heart of the matter. I suppose it's my way of asking you what *your* view of Christianity is. Sorry to be morbid, but if you were to die tonight and you found yourself standing before God and he asked, 'Why should I let you into heaven?', what would you reply? Don't go on to the next paragraph until you've written down your answer.

According to the Bible, answers to this question always fall neatly into one of two categories: 'the right answer', or 'the wrong answers'.

The wrong answers

Let's take the wrong ones first. The wrong answers are those which place confidence in what *I am*, or what *I have done*. So if you've written, 'God, you should let me into heaven because I...', I'm afraid you're on to a loser. You may have done lots of good things. Perhaps you've written something like, 'Let me in, God, because I've been pretty good on the whole. I'm a good person – I don't steal, I don't lie (well not unless I absolutely have to), I give to charity. I've certainly never killed anyone. Actually, there are *loads* of people worse than me. I've kept the Ten Commandments, I try to live by Jesus' Sermon on the Mount, I pay my taxes, I don't cut queues. Other people like having me around, God, so I imagine you will too.' But that's a wrong answer. In a similar vein, one person actually said to me, 'Look, Rico, how can you say that I won't be allowed in to heaven? I mean, I give blood and everything. I give *blood*, Rico.'

Or perhaps you've written the kind of thing that my friend's wife from the dinner party would have written: 'God, you should let me in because I've always prayed to you when I needed you. I'm sure you won't let me down now.' She would probably echo the words of Catherine the Great, who said, 'God will forgive me. That's his job.'

Another wrong answer is the religious one. You may be relying on your religious habits to get you into heaven. So perhaps you've written something like this: 'God, you should let me in because I go to church. Not only that, but I'm a member of the Church of England. I never take your name in vain, and when others do, I strongly disapprove. I do good things in the community. Furthermore, I've been baptized. I've been confirmed. I go to communion. I even sing in the choir. Not to mention the fact that I pray *and* read the Bible. Sometimes regularly. And there aren't many people you can say that about in this day and age.' You're right that you're in a minority. But it's still a wrong answer. If you have written something like that, then can I say to you categorically that doing these religious things will *not* enable you to enter heaven. Again and again, Jesus taught that religious observance has no power to save people. If you are putting your confidence here, then please don't – because you've been misled.

Now why is it that trusting in these good things counts for nothing when it comes to healing your relationship with God? Because, as we've already seen, Jesus insists that our problem is deep within us, in our 'hearts'. It is this 'heart', says Jesus, that is corrupt.

That's the problem with the human condition. In my world, I'm the centre of the universe. I instinctively think of everything in terms of how it relates to me, not in terms of how it relates to the God who made me. It's natural for human beings to think and act in this way, but the Bible says that, although it's natural, it isn't how we were made to be. Indeed, it's the reason why the world is as imperfect as it is.

So my good deeds – whether it's going to church or giving to charity or treating others as I would like to be treated myself or whatever – are like small sticking plasters on a gaping wound. They're fine in and of themselves, but they cannot cure the problem that keeps me from God.

Hang on – I know lots of good people. Selfless, loving people who continually do lots of good things for those around them. Are you saying that these people are destined to be punished by God? But it makes no difference how good our deeds are: it is not so much *what we do* that is the problem, it is *what we are*. Our good deeds cannot get us into heaven any more than our bad deeds condemn us to hell. It is what we *are* that sets us against God.

Again, let me stress that there is nothing wrong with good deeds. They only become dangerous when, like the Pharisees and teachers of the law, I delude myself into thinking that they are the means by which I put myself on a good footing with God. These religious authorities had already decided the criteria by which God would accept them. They kept their own rules and traditions. Getting God to accept them meant attending to *external* details: for example, they were to wash in special ways and avoid eating certain things. It was all about outward ritual and had nothing to do with our inner problem: the self-centredness of the human heart. That's why Jesus says this about them:

> 'These people honour me with their lips, but their hearts are far from me. They worship me in vain; their teachings are but rules taught by men.'[1]

It is so much easier to concentrate on the outside appearance, to stick on a few plasters, rather than face up to what is within. And Jesus insists that no amount of religious tradition or morality or Bible-reading or 'turning over of new leaves' can bring our hearts any closer to God. Remember that, as Jesus points out in Mark chapter 7, our hearts are – and always will be, no matter what we do – fountains of evil:

---

[1] Mark chapter 7 verses 6-7

'What comes out of a man is what makes him "unclean". For from within, out of men's hearts, come evil thoughts, sexual immorality, theft, murder, adultery, greed, malice, deceit, lewdness, envy, slander, arrogance and folly. All these evils come from inside and make a man "unclean".'

Even Paul, one of the most effective Christian workers in history, lamented the state of his heart when he wrote in Romans chapter 7 verse 19: 'For what I do is not the good I want to do; no, the evil I do not want to do – this I keep on doing.' Jesus' words about the evil of the human heart are as true for Paul as they are for us. Can we, with the Pharisees, hope that the good things we do will cover over the evil in our hearts? No – according to Jesus, that is the wrong answer. *There is, in fact, nothing I can do to save myself.*

The right answer

Wonderfully, however, that is not the end of the story. There is a right answer to God's question, 'Why should I let you into heaven?' According to the Bible, the right answer has to do with God's *grace*. The right answer is something like this: 'God, you should let me in to heaven because of what Christ has done. He died on the cross so that I could be forgiven for my sin. He was abandoned so that I could be accepted.' In other words, it's not about the good things we've done for God, but rather it's about the good thing *Christ has done for us*. We don't have to earn anything.

The film *Saving Private Ryan*, set during World War II, tells the story of a group of men who are given orders to rescue a single man from behind enemy lines in

Normandy. Why is the man so important? We are told that his three brothers have all recently been killed in action, leaving him as the only child of a single mother. When the US Army Chief of Staff hears about the situation, he gives orders to protect this precious remaining son, Private James Ryan, and he sends out a team of soldiers to bring him back alive.

The rescue mission is extremely perilous, and it claims the lives of the soldiers, one after the other. At one point the Captain says, 'This Ryan had better be worth it. He'd better go home, cure some disease or invent the longer-lasting light bulb.' But they obey the orders to rescue Ryan. And in the final battle scene, set on a heavily-shelled bridge, as the Captain himself dies, he whispers his last words to a dumbstruck Private Ryan: *'James – earn this – earn it.'*

Fifty years pass, and in the closing shots of the film we see an elderly James Ryan returning to Normandy with his wife, children and grandchildren. He kneels beside the grave of the Captain and, as tears fill his eyes, he says, 'My family is with me today... Every day I think about what you said to me that day on the bridge. I've tried to live my life the best I could. I hope that was enough. I hope that at least in your eyes I've earned what all of you have done for me.' Then he turns to his wife and asks with some anxiety, 'Tell me I've led a good life... Tell me I'm a good man...'

It is clear that Private Ryan has lived his entire life with the last words of his rescuer ringing in his ears. *Earn this – earn it*. In a way, the words have crippled him. Could he ever live up to the deaths of those young men? As one soldier says earlier in the film: 'Do the mothers of the men who died to rescue him think he has earned their sons' deaths?'

The Captain's last words were *'Earn it.'* But Jesus' last words – recorded in John's Gospel – were *'It is finished.'* They, too, are words that will remain with me every day of my life. In the original language, Greek, Jesus' phrase is a single word, *tetelesti*. Literally, it means, 'It is complete.' This is not a desperate cry of self-pity – not *I* am finished, but *it* is finished. It's the word a builder might use as he places the last roof slate on a new house. Or something a couple might say when they finally pay off their mortgage after 25 years. *Tetelesti:* the debt is paid, it is done, it is finished.

So, unlike the life of James Ryan, which was weighed down by the attempt to somehow earn the deaths of those who saved him, the life of the Christian is marked by freedom. As he died to save my life, Jesus didn't ask me to earn it. And he didn't say that the worthiness of my life depends upon the good things I may have done. No. He said, 'Rico, it is finished. All your sin – past, present, future – is forgiven. I've paid off your debts.' He doesn't ask me to earn it because he knows I never can, and he tells me *'It is finished'* even though he knows that in the future my life won't be perfect, however hard I try.

And that's what grace is. It's God behaving towards us in a way we simply do not deserve. When we look at what happened at the cross, we see God graciously reaching out to us, offering us something that we haven't paid for, don't need to pay for, and in fact cannot pay for. 2 Corinthians chapter 5 verse 21 says that, 'God made him who had no sin to be sin for us, so that in him we might become the righteousness of God.' This is an amazing exchange: Jesus takes on board our sin, and we take on board his righteousness. That's the only reason we can be accepted by God.

Let me paint a little scenario at this point. It's not the most elegant of metaphors, but I hope it helps. Let's say you're on your way to the local shop when you see the fifteen-year-old who lives down the street in the process of 'borrowing' his parents' car. You know he doesn't have a licence, but he is nevertheless backing it out of their driveway in what the police would call 'a rushed and careless fashion'. You then watch the car swerving all over the road. As the car reaches your house it spins out of control, ploughs through your lovingly-fashioned privet hedge, flattens an attractive ornamental fence and takes out the drainpipe near your front door. All you've been able to do is watch in horror as this little tableau unfurls in front of you. Hopefully, as he gets out of the car sheepishly, you resist the urge to physically assault him. The dust settles and he meets your gaze. At that point you have three options.

Option 1: Justice
The first option open to you is *justice*. Give him exactly what his deeds deserve. So you tell him, 'I'm going to call the police. I'm going to cite you for driving without a licence, and I'm going to have you breathalized. Then we'll call your parents, and we'll see what they have to say about it. And by the way, you'll have to get a job too, because that hedge needs sorting, as does my fence, and the drainpipe.' That would be justice: you're not being excessive, you're simply giving him what he deserves. No more, no less.

Option 2: Moderation

The second option is *moderation*. Moderation is giving him a little bit less than he deserves. So you say, 'Look, I'm not going to call the police, but I am going to call your parents and we are going to establish exactly what the hedge, fence and drainpipe will cost to fix. You'll have to pay for the damage, but it won't go any further.' If you choose this option, the fifteen-year-old should be very thankful – because he is getting less of a punishment than he deserves.

Then there is a third option. But I'm not sure I should suggest it because you'll probably think it's irrational and scandalous, perhaps even naive and stupid. You'd be right in thinking that it's not common sense, and it could blow up in your face, but here it is: you could treat the fifteen-year-old with *grace*.

Option 3: Grace

You could say, 'Look, you've messed up. You mowed down my privet, my attractive ornamental fence and you destroyed my drainpipe. Despite that, I'm not going to call the police. In fact I'm not even sure I want to get you into trouble with your family. As for the privet, the fence and the drainpipe, well, I can fix those. Why don't you get the car off the lawn, then we'll sit and have a chat, so I can find out how I can help you.' You could do that. The only condition you place is, 'Please reverse the car out of my front garden.'

What do you think about that? You might think, 'That is the stupidest thing I've ever heard. All the kid's going to do is joyride the next day, and he's going to smash someone else's fence down or worse.' You could be right.

That is the risk. That is the scandal of grace. But it is also possible that grace would touch that young boy's life to the deepest part of his soul. Your generosity, your interest in his welfare and his future could unlock his potential and turn him around. You could see the transformation of a life as he receives an utterly undeserved gift, as he is touched by unconditional love and seeks to live in gratitude to you for your kindness. Option three is outrageous, yes. Irrational, most likely. But it could be utterly liberating for the boy.

A good illustration of that truth is the character of Valjean, in Victor Hugo's novel *Les Misérables* (which was made into the hugely successful musical of the same name). After serving 19 years of hard labour for stealing bread (five for the actual theft and the rest for subsequent escape attempts), Jean Valjean has become a hardened, bitter man who is feared by everyone. On his release from prison, he finds it impossible to find work or shelter. The paper he is required to show tells everyone that he is a prisoner on parole, and no one wants anything to do with him. Finally, a kindly bishop takes him into his home, offering him food and a place to sleep.

Valjean betrays his trust, however, and steals some of the family silver while the household is asleep. He is quickly caught by three constables and brought back to the bishop's house. Things look desperate for Valjean. The bishop has the opportunity to incriminate him for his act of betrayal and have him imprisoned for the rest of his life. Instead, the bishop says this: 'So, here you are! I'm delighted to see you. Had you forgotten that I gave you the candlesticks as well? They're silver like the rest, and worth a good 200 francs. Did you forget to take them?'

So the constables let him go. After they've gone, the bishop insists that Valjean keep the candlesticks, and tells him, 'Do not forget, do not ever forget, that you have promised me to use the money to make yourself an honest man.' Valjean is so moved by the grace of the bishop that he is transformed.

Like Valjean, we are utterly guilty and have no resources to pay for what we've done. In fact, as Jesus says, we deserve to be 'thrown into hell'. Unless we see ourselves in that dire state, we won't see the amazing generosity of God's gift: the gift of his only Son, dying a terrible death on a cross – for us. And we won't allow ourselves to be transformed by God's extraordinary love for us.

The novel also portrays a character called Javert, a police inspector who pursues Valjean for years, consumed by his desire for justice, and wanting to punish Valjean. But Javert's idea of justice leaves no room for compassion, or forgiveness. There is no *grace* in him. However, the grace shown to Valjean by the bishop means that, contrary to all expectations, Valjean eventually saves Javert's life. The ultimate destinies of the two characters could not be further removed: Valjean has clearly been transformed by grace, but Javert – fatally unsettled by this 'grace' that goes against his every instinct – throws himself from a bridge and drowns in the Seine.

Perhaps the best summary of grace in the Bible is what Paul writes in Ephesians chapter 2 verses 8 and 9:

> For it is by grace you have been saved, through faith – and this not from yourselves, it is the gift of God – not by works, so that no-one can boast.

So Paul says here, 'Look, you've been saved from eternal punishment by Jesus' death on a cross. And that's a free gift. Nothing you've done, nothing you might boast about, has earned this gift. It's been given to you regardless of anything good or bad you may have done in your lives.' And that brings us around again to the right answer to the question, 'Why should God let you into heaven?': 'I should be allowed into heaven because I've put my trust in what Jesus did for me on the cross.'

Of course, we can only say that when we realize that we are powerless to save ourselves, when we turn to God in utter dependence and weakness, recognizing that nothing *we do* will be enough to cure the problem of the human heart.

Unsurprisingly, some people find it very difficult not only to admit how weak and dependent they are, but also to accept that anything so costly could be given to them for free. It *is* difficult to accept this gift from God when all our lives we've been taught that we have to earn our supper, earn our praise, earn our salary. But the truth is that the Christian life is not about duty. It's about receiving a gift I don't deserve, and then living a life of thanks for that gift.

And we know that as soon as we accept that gift, we will have eternal life in heaven. We are accepted by God. But what happens in the meantime?

What does grace mean *now*?
Victor Hugo wrote, 'Life's greatest happiness is to be convinced we are loved.' Because of the cross, Christians are convinced that they are loved. The cross makes one thing very clear: I am loved unconditionally, because even

though he knows what I'm like, Christ still died on my behalf. The very person who will ultimately judge the world loves me completely and unalterably.

What greater proof of love could there be than to die for someone? And Christ has done that for me. As Paul says in Romans chapter 5 verses 7 and 8:

> Very rarely will anyone die for a righteous man, though for a good man someone might possibly dare to die. But God demonstrates his own love for us in this: while we were still sinners, Christ died for us.

Although we are more sinful than we ever realized, we are more loved than we ever dreamed.

My young nephews, Dalton (six) and Patrick (two and a half), enjoy nothing better on my days off at home than to have me teach them basic rugby technique – usually in the living room. We were doing this a while back, and Patrick got so excited by the whole thing that, as I was scrummaging with his brother, he picked up a large flowerpot and proudly marched around the room with it. By the time I looked up, the room was covered in soil. My mother opened the door and found that her carpet had been turned into a playing field. She looked at Patrick and his plant pot, walked over to him, replaced the pot, picked him up, kissed him and said, 'Let's go and have some lunch.' As you can see, he didn't deserve to be treated like that (and nor did I, to be frank). But as the two of them left the room, I could see how thrilled little Patrick was. You see, he knew that he was loved unconditionally. And he's a very secure, very contented child who actually now longs to please my mother whenever he comes to stay.

This unconditional love means three things:

1. There are no masks to wear

My mother knows exactly what Patrick is like, but she loves him anyway. God knows exactly what I'm like, and yet he still loves me. *That means I don't have to pretend with God.* There's no hiding behind masks. The writer Somerset Maugham noted with rueful irony that 'human nature is not only as bad as it can be, but a great deal worse'. Despite that fact, which God well knows, he unconditionally loves us.

Dietrich Bonhoeffer was a German pastor who was killed by the Nazis. He wrote these words:

> Complete truthfulness is only possible where sin has been uncovered and forgiven by Jesus. The cross is God's truth about us and, therefore, it is the only power which can make us truthful. When we know the cross, we are no longer afraid of the truth.

It's an extraordinary relief to no longer have to hide the truth about ourselves.

2. There is nothing to prove

There is, as best-selling author Philip Yancey says, 'nothing I can do to make God love me more, and there is nothing I can do to make him love me less'. That makes a huge difference to my life, because I live in a culture of conditional love. My mother's love for Patrick is unconditional, but when he goes to school he will be loved *conditionally*. He will constantly hear this message: 'If you perform, we will love you. But if you don't perform, we will withdraw that love.' And that can be crippling to human beings.

I think that's one of the reasons why modern society is

so *driven*. We are very, very competitive because we are aware of this ceaseless ranking that is going on all around us. We'll feel loved if only we could be younger, fitter, more successful, more beautiful, more talented, a bit thinner, harder-working and so on. People are often conditioned by the belief that unless I win, I won't be loved – so I'd better make sure I win.

I once spoke at a school that displayed only two boards on which they honoured ex-pupils. On one was a list of Olympic gold medallists. On the other was a list of Nobel Prize winners. Well, I don't know about you, but I'm not going to make it onto that kind of roll call. So there is amazing joy and freedom when I realize that grace means God loves me anyway, gold medal or not.

3. There are no grudges to bear

God's grace deals with my bitterness even though I may feel deeply hurt by another person. The desire for revenge may be perfectly understandable. But when I think about what I myself have been forgiven by God, I feel much less able to hold on to grudges, bitterness and hatred. And this, too, is an extraordinary relief. Jesus gives an illustration in Luke chapter 7 verses 41 to 43, which makes this point exactly:

> 'Two men owed money to a certain moneylender. One owed him five hundred denarii, and the other fifty. Neither of them had the money to pay him back, so he cancelled the debts of both. Now which of them will love him more?'
>
> Simon replied, 'I suppose the one who had the bigger debt cancelled.'
>
> 'You have judged correctly,' Jesus said.

When we realize how much we've been forgiven, we love God, and forgive others, all the more.

So this is grace: God sending Christ to die on the cross so that I can be forgiven, even though I've done nothing to earn it, even though I deserve punishment. In the light of that, there is no need to pretend we're something we're not or boast about what we've achieved, and there is every reason to freely forgive those who do us wrong.

Raging Bull is the autobiography of American boxer Jake La Motta, which was made into an Oscar-winning film starring Robert De Niro. Raised in New York slums by a father who beat both him and his mother, crime was La Motta's life: he stole, raped and murdered. Following several terms in prison, he developed into a savage fighter who became Middleweight Champion of the World at the age of twenty-seven, the hero to thousands. The relationship he had with his wife was just as violent as the one between his own mother and father, and throughout his life he was particularly tortured by the guilty memory of a man he had once beaten to death.

Even though he has seen Jake viciously assault three prison guards, Joseph, the chaplain at La Motta's first prison, tries to befriend him. He understands that Jake – like all human beings – needs forgiveness. On the day Jake is set to leave, he goes to say a grateful goodbye to Joseph in the prison chapel. And as he does so, he is seized by the urge to tell Joseph about the man he killed.

I could feel myself sweating again, and Father Joseph looked at me with that curious expression of his like he knew a lot more than I thought he knew, and he said to me, very softly, 'Jake, is there something you want to tell me? Something else that I don't know? You know I've never tried to trap you, but don't try to keep things bottled up inside you forever. Guilt is a complex thing, Jake – I think you're too young to realize it, but slowly it begins to make you hate yourself because you know you've done something wrong, no matter whether anyone else knows it, and that forces you to know that you're not the man people think you are, and after a while it makes you begin to hate other people, everyone you meet, because they assume that you're better than you are, which is only more of a reproach to you. Don't try to keep things bottled up forever. If you feel this way, don't let these feelings consume you… I've never probed at you, Jake, but I see that something is troubling you. Trust me. Let me help you. Have faith in me.'

He saw how I was standing without moving, then he gestured to the altar again and said, 'Or if you can't have faith in me at least have faith in Him. Tell Him what's troubling you, Jake, and ask his forgiveness. Ask Him to set your feet on the right path. Jake, you've got to trust someone.'

There it was again. I felt like screaming at him, *You don't know what it is! You don't know how bad it is! You don't understand!* But I knew that would blow it, and suddenly I couldn't take it any longer. I said in a low, strangled voice, 'You don't understand how it is. I can't trust anybody, I never learned how…'

And suddenly I was afraid to stay there another second, so I said good-bye and turned and ran out of the chapel.

There is a way to be forgiven for the things we've done which we know are wrong. There is a way to be free from the kind of guilt Jake La Motta felt. But it requires us to take the step Jake La Motta could not take: it requires us to stop running away from what we fear, and trust someone. I bet you know by now who that is.

06

Jesus – His Resurrection

If Jesus had not apparently risen from the dead, we probably wouldn't even have heard of him. But his resurrection changes everything. As we've seen, God sent Jesus to die on a cross because of our sin. If Christ's death on the cross brings us forgiveness, what does his subsequent resurrection add to that? Let me ask you a question to get the ball rolling: 'How do you know for certain that you have eternal life?'

Funerals of young people are always particularly moving, and the first one I ever took was for a musician called Stuart Spencer. He died of cancer in his thirties. He was a deeply committed Christian, however, so the tone of our final meeting, just three days before he died, was much calmer than you'd expect. Nevertheless, I was emotional, and I blurted out what was on my mind. (It was one of those moments where immediately afterwards you think to yourself, 'Did I just say that *out loud?*') I said to him, 'Stuart, what's it like to die?' His answer was as simple as it was unexpected: 'Rico, Christ has risen from the dead.'

1 Thessalonians chapter 4 verse 14 explains that just as Christ died and rose again, so Christians, when they die, will rise again:

> We believe that Jesus died and rose again and so we believe that God will bring with Jesus those who have fallen asleep in him.

Paul elaborates in Romans chapter 5 verse 10:

> For if, when we were God's enemies, we were reconciled to
> him through the death of his Son, how much more, having
> been reconciled, shall we be saved through his life!

In other words, if Christ's death achieved our
reconciliation with God, just imagine what Christ's
resurrection has achieved for us.

Stuart knew what he had to look forward to beyond
death. 1 Corinthians chapter 2 verse 9 says that 'No eye
has seen, no ear has heard, no mind has conceived what
God has prepared for those who love him.' So as he died,
Stuart was filled with hope. Not empty, wish-upon-a-star
hope, but hope founded on the reality of Jesus'
resurrection.

How could he have been so sure of something that
happened two thousand years ago?

The death was certain

At the end of his account of the crucifixion in chapter 15,
Mark homes in on three women who have watched the
whole gruesome ordeal:

> Some women were watching [the crucifixion] from a distance.
> Among them were Mary Magdalene, Mary the mother of James
> the younger and of Joses, and Salome. In Galilee these women
> had followed him and cared for his needs. Many other women
> who had come up with him to Jerusalem were also there.

Not only have they watched Jesus die, but two of them
also watch him being buried: 'Mary Magdalene and
Mary the mother of Joses saw where he was laid.' They
are witnesses of his death, a death made all the more

tragic because of his youth: Jesus was in his early thirties when he was killed.

If we are in any doubt about the certainty of his death, Mark goes on to tell us:

> It was Preparation Day (that is, the day before the Sabbath). So as evening approached, Joseph of Arimathea, a prominent member of the Council, who was himself waiting for the kingdom of God, went boldly to Pilate and asked for Jesus' body. Pilate was surprised to hear that he was already dead. Summoning the centurion, he asked him if Jesus had already died. When he learned from the centurion that it was so, he gave the body to Joseph.

It was unusual for crucifixion to result in death so quickly, so the Roman governor Pontius Pilate queries the centurion, the same centurion who had stood only a short distance from the cross and watched the extraordinary way in which Jesus had died. The centurion confirms that yes, Jesus had indeed already died.

The Romans had many talents, but when it came to killing people, they were experts. In chapter 19 of John's Gospel, we're told that because it was the day before their holy day, the Jews did not want bodies left on crosses. As a result, they ask Pilate to have the legs of the condemned broken in order to hasten their deaths (the only way you can breathe on a cross is if you keep pushing yourself up with your legs). Soldiers are duly despatched to do this, and they break the legs of the two criminals crucified with Jesus. But when they come to Jesus they find that he is 'already dead', so there is no need to break any bones. 'Instead,' we are told, 'one of the soldiers pierced Jesus' side with a spear, bringing a sudden flow of blood and water.' Why bother lancing him in this way? Perhaps it was sheer brutality but, whatever the reason, the 'flow of blood and water' also suggests that Jesus was dead: the blood coagulates when we die, leaving the water to separate away from the blood. (That Jesus would not suffer any broken bones – an extremely unusual fact given these circumstances – is predicted a number of times in sections of the Bible written hundreds of years previously.)

Having established that Jesus is dead, Pilate gives Joseph permission to remove the body from the cross:

> So Joseph bought some linen cloth, took down the body, wrapped it in the linen, and placed it in a tomb cut out of rock. Then he rolled a stone against the entrance of the tomb.

In other words, Pontius Pilate, the centurion, the Roman soldiers, Joseph of Arimathea and the women were absolutely certain that *Jesus had died*. There's no doubt about it. All the evidence points to the conclusion that Jesus was dead.

The tomb was empty

We are told in Matthew's Gospel that the next day (the Sabbath), in addition to the large stone placed over the entrance, a seal was placed upon the tomb. (This was because some of the religious leaders feared that the disciples would steal the body and then pretend that Jesus had come back from the dead.) People knew that to break such a seal resulted in execution. Further security was provided in the form of a Roman guard, deployed to ensure that no one tampered with the tomb. Equally, the guards knew that to fail in their duty meant immediate execution.

Once the Jewish holy day is over, the women return to

the tomb that they had watched Jesus being buried in just 36 hours earlier. They don't go hoping that Jesus might be alive, they go expecting to find a corpse. Mark chapter 16 verses 1 to 3:

> When the Sabbath was over, Mary Magdalene, Mary the mother of James, and Salome bought spices so that they might go to anoint Jesus' body. Very early on the first day of the week, just after sunrise, they were on their way to the tomb and they asked each other, 'Who will roll the stone away from the entrance of the tomb?'

And then the women are subjected to three shocks of escalating intensity.

The first shock comes when they find that their concern over who will roll the stone away is irrelevant:

> But when they looked up, they saw that the stone, which was very large, had been rolled away.

There is no need to fret about the stone, because divine power has dealt with it.

Then comes the second shock, as they go inside the tomb:

> As they entered the tomb, they saw a young man dressed in a white robe sitting on the right side, and they were alarmed.

They see a man whose appearance is so striking ('like lightning', according to Matthew) that it causes the Roman guard posted to the tomb to shake (Matthew tells us that they become 'like dead men'). The women, understandably, are terrified. But they are not delusional – the man affirms the reality of what is happening:

'Don't be alarmed,' he said. 'You are looking for Jesus the Nazarene, who was crucified.'

Yes, the man from Nazareth, the one you've been following these past three years, was killed.

'See the place where they laid him.'

He was really buried here, you don't have the wrong address. The fact is that Jesus simply isn't here any more. (As for the guards' reaction, Matthew tells us this: '...some of the guards went into the city and reported to the chief priests everything that had happened. When the chief priests had met with the elders and devised a plan, they gave the soldiers a large sum of money, telling them, "You are to say, 'His disciples came during the night and stole him away while we were asleep.' If this report gets to the governor, we will satisfy him and keep you out of trouble." So the soldiers took the money and did as they were instructed.')

But the third shock will change the women's lives forever.

The body was resurrected
This third shock, the biggest of them all, comes as the young man in the empty tomb tells them the reason why Jesus' body is not there:

'He has risen!'

Just as there was no need for their concern about the stone, there is now no need for the spices they'd brought to anoint the corpse. Divine power has not only flung the stone away, it has raised a body to life. The reason the tomb is empty is because Jesus isn't dead any more. He is alive. This is a historical fact – the kind of fact you can be sure about. The kind of fact you can rely on. *Three days after his execution, Jesus rose from the dead.* Dr Simon Greenleaf, the celebrated Royal Professor of Law at Harvard University, who was famously sceptical of Christianity, was challenged to evaluate the resurrection of Jesus using well-established legal principles. He wrote this: 'According to the laws of legal evidence, the resurrection of Jesus Christ is proven by more substantial evidence than any other event of ancient history.'[1]

You could argue that those three words – 'He has risen!' – are the most influential ever spoken. The four Gospels record several different reactions to this staggering statement. As the women heard about Jesus' resurrection before anyone else, let's look firstly at how they respond.

Reaction 1: The women

So shocking is the messenger and his revelation that they *run*.

> Trembling and bewildered, the women went out and fled from the tomb. They said nothing to anyone, because they were afraid.

Despite the man's instructions ('…go, tell his disciples and Peter, "He is going ahead of you into Galilee. There you will see him, just as he told you."'), at first the women don't say anything to anyone. Why? Because 'they were afraid'. They are 'trembling and bewildered'.

But Mark insists that they shouldn't be. Look again at Mark chapter 16 verse 7: '…go, tell his disciples and Peter, "He is going ahead of you into Galilee. There you will see him, *just as he told you.*"' I put that last phrase in italics, just

---

[1] Greenleaf, S., *The Testimony of the Evangelists: The Four Gospels Examined by the Rules of Evidence* (Grand Rapids: Kregel Publications, 1995).

in case you missed it. Mark reminds us by recording those words that the women shouldn't have been surprised by the resurrection. Jesus had taught them repeatedly that he would suffer, die and rise again. Mark chapter 8: 'The Son of Man must be killed and after three days rise again.' Mark chapter 9: 'They will kill him, and after three days he will rise.' Mark chapter 10: 'The Gentiles will mock him and spit on him, flog him and kill him. Three days later he will rise.' Jesus is always in control. He knows exactly the manner of his death and what will happen to him beyond death, and he explains everything to them before it happens.

Because they have not understood what Jesus came to do – to suffer, die and rise from death – and because they have not understood that following Christ is not just about what happens this side of death, the women are afraid. Mark is telling us that our understanding of the resurrection is crucial. If we don't get it, we'll go away bewildered and afraid, just like the women.

Reaction 2: Peter and John

After the women tell the disciples what they've seen, we learn from John that he and Peter run to the tomb to see for themselves. (Although he is writing about himself, John refers to himself as 'the other disciple'.) As you might expect, this passage – taken from John chapter 20 – is full of very specific eyewitness detail:

> So Peter and the other disciple started for the tomb. Both were running, but the other disciple outran Peter and reached the tomb first. He bent over and looked in at the strips of linen lying there but did not go in. Then Simon Peter, who was behind him, arrived and went into the tomb. He saw the strips of linen lying there, as well as the burial cloth that had been around Jesus'

> head. The cloth was folded up by itself, separate from the linen. Finally the other disciple, who had reached the tomb first, also went inside. He saw and believed. (They still did not understand from Scripture that Jesus had to rise from the dead.)

So what is it that they 'believed'? John makes a point of telling us that neither of them understood 'from Scripture' (that is, from the Bible) that Jesus had to be resurrected, so they don't yet believe that Jesus has risen from the dead. No, all they believe is that the tomb is empty. And there are many people today who would share Peter and John's belief at this point: Jesus died, was buried, the tomb was empty for whatever reason, Jesus' body was indeed gone. But they don't accept anything beyond that.

Later, after Jesus has physically appeared to some of them, the disciples finally believe that Jesus had indeed risen from the dead, that everything he had told them to expect had come to pass. Well, most of them believe. All except one, in fact.

Reaction 3: Thomas

Then John records a wonderful incident. We read about one of the disciples – a man called Thomas – who refuses to believe that Jesus has risen. The other disciples tell Thomas that they've seen Jesus. But Thomas knows that dead people don't come back. He insists not only on seeing Jesus for himself, but also on touching him, as if to prove that this vision is some kind of ghost or communal hallucination:

> Now Thomas (called Didymus), one of the Twelve, was not with the disciples when Jesus came. So the other disciples told him, 'We have seen the Lord!'

> But he said to them, 'Unless I see the nail marks in his hands and put my finger where the nails were, and put my hand into his side, I will not believe it.'

So Thomas needs evidence of the sledgehammer variety. He says, 'Unless I touch his open wounds, I'm not going to believe it'. And of course he wouldn't offer to go poking around in someone else's open wounds unless he was certain that it wasn't going to happen. I trust that if you visit a sick friend in hospital, you don't ask to poke around in their wounds. If you do, you're sicker than your friend. But Thomas was about to be transformed by seeing the risen Christ:

> A week later his disciples were in the house again, and Thomas was with them. Though the doors were locked, Jesus came and stood among them and said, 'Peace be with you!' Then he said to Thomas, 'Put your finger here; see my hands. Reach out your hand and put it into my side. Stop doubting and believe.'

Thomas then makes one of the greatest statements of belief in the Bible:

> 'My Lord and my God!'

Thirty years later, this stubborn, rational, incredulous man was to die a martyr's death testifying to what he had seen.

The Gospels alone tell us of 11 separate instances in which Jesus is seen after his death – at different times and in different places, to different people. In 1 Corinthians chapter 15, Paul tells us that over five hundred people saw Jesus at one time, many of whom were still living when Paul was writing. So Paul was saying to his readers, 'If you don't believe me, go and talk to the eyewitnesses. They're still alive and will confirm the truth of what I'm saying.' The sightings are too many and too varied for us to reach any other conclusion than that Jesus rose from the dead.

So we're left with some sobering and irresistible facts. Firstly, Jesus died and was buried. Second, the tomb was empty. Third, Jesus was seen alive by hundreds of people, many of whom were later to die insisting on the truth of Jesus' resurrection. How many of us would be prepared to face a slow and painful execution for what we knew was a lie?

We've seen how Thomas, Peter, John and the women reacted, but what is *our* reaction to these events? If we become convinced of the reality of the resurrection, there are two important conclusions for us to draw.

A great hope

The first conclusion is that the resurrection gives us certain hope. Why? Because it means we can confidently put our trust in the person who said this:

> 'I am the resurrection and the life. He who believes in me will live, even though he dies; and whoever lives and believes in me will never die.'[2]

The resurrection conclusively demonstrates Jesus' power and authority over death – not just over his own, but also over ours.

Those words in Mark chapter 16 verse 6 – 'He is risen!' – are words that can dissolve our fear of death. Indeed, they are the words upon which Christianity was built, words which transformed a sad and fearful group of

[2] John chapter 11 verses 25-26

disciples into men so fearless that they would die for what they knew to be true: Jesus had risen. And indeed, nearly all of them *were* executed precisely because of their insistence on that single fact.

As Paul writes in 1 Corinthians chapter 15 verse 14: 'if Christ has not been raised, our preaching is useless and so is your faith'. Why would it be 'useless'? Because if the resurrection had never happened, we might conclude, as some people do, that Christ was just a man. 'Great teacher, great healer, great miracle-worker. But it was a shame he couldn't make good his promise that he would die, then rise again three days later...' If Christ had not risen from the dead, how would we ever know that the price for our rebellion had been successfully paid? The question I asked you at the beginning of the chapter – 'How do you know for certain that you have eternal life?' – was a tough one. But you *can* be certain. The proof is in the resurrection.

Stuart Spencer and I had become close friends, so I was honoured when he asked if I would speak at his funeral. Many of his friends came to the funeral, and many were not followers of Christ. They came, they heard about Jesus' resurrection from death and, as far as I could tell, all but one walked away untouched. And that reminds us that although the resurrection is a great hope for those who follow Christ, it is also a great warning for those who ignore him.

A great warning
One song that takes me back to my school days is John Lennon's *Imagine*. It's a brilliant song, with memorable words expressing wistful longing for a happy life now, with nothing beyond it to trouble us. Lennon knows that death,

and all its attendant uncertainty, is a cloud over our lives.

Brilliant though it is, Lennon's song remains – appropriately enough – a work of pure imagination. Those words in Mark – 'He is risen!' – show us that there is life beyond the grave. We could live for today, as John Lennon suggests we should, but that would be to ignore a great warning provided by the resurrection: this life is not all there is. Death is not the end. But whereas many will be raised to life, many will also be raised to face a judgement that they cannot possibly bear. The thought of a day of judgement is extremely distressing, especially if – like me – you fear for loved ones. But, in fact, judgement is a very good thing indeed – and the alternative to judgement is absolutely appalling.

In 1994, the film Schindler's List was released. One episode of the story is set in and around Krakow in Poland during World War II. SS guards are moving the Jews from their town ghetto to a labour camp outside and Oscar Schindler, the hero of the story, sees a mother and her son brutally murdered by the guards. What shocks Schindler most is the fact that this murder has taken place in full view of a young girl who is about three years old. He notices her because she is dressed in red. In the book that inspired the film, the author continues:

> Later in the day after he'd absorbed a ration of brandy, Oscar understood the proposition in its clearest terms: they permitted witnesses, such witnesses as the red toddler, because they believed all the witnesses would perish too.

The Nazi guards did what they liked because they believed that they would never be called to account for their actions. The little girl in red could be allowed to witness the murder because she wouldn't be living much longer anyway. In effect, nothing they did mattered any more. All those with the power to condemn their actions would be dead.

But death is not the end. Thankfully, the Bible repeatedly assures us that wrongdoing will not be left unaddressed – ultimately there will be justice. As it says in Hebrews chapter 9 verse 27: '...man is destined to die once, and after that to face judgement'. Do any of us really want to live in a world where nothing matters, where even the most extreme cruelty is met with vacuous silence? Jesus' resurrection is a wonderful assurance that justice will eventually be done: 'For he [God] has set a day when he will judge the world with justice by the man he has appointed' (Paul, speaking in Acts chapter 17, verse 31). And who is this 'appointed' man? The resurrection confirms the answer. It is God's only Son, a man who knows all about Thomas's doubts before he even speaks, a man who knows all about *us* and yet still gave up his life for us.

Paul preached that message to the people of Athens, telling them that, ultimately, God will judge everyone, and that he 'has given proof of this to all men by raising him [Jesus] from the dead'. No one likes being told about judgement, so how do these people react?

> When they heard about the resurrection of the dead, some of them sneered, but others said, 'We want to hear you again on this subject.' At that, Paul left the Council. A few men became followers of Paul and believed.

Some of them sneered, while some wanted to hear more on the subject. We also read that some believed. What about you?

07

What Is A Christian?

A little boy at Sunday School is asked to draw a picture of Mary, Joseph and the baby Jesus in the midst of their flight into Egypt. (The teacher had been telling them about the time in Matthew chapter 2, when an angel appears to Joseph in a dream and warns him to flee with his family from the murderous King Herod). So the little boy carefully draws a picture of a huge aeroplane and when the teacher asks him what it is, he points out that it's 'the flight into Egypt', indicating Joseph, Mary and the baby Jesus, who are sitting happily in the passenger seats. 'But who's that?' asks the teacher, pointing to a shadowy figure in the cockpit. Growing a bit tired of all the stupid questions, the little boy says, 'That's Pontius Pilot.'

It's not only five-year-olds who misunderstand what Christianity's about. There must be millions of people in the United Kingdom alone who have rejected what they *think* is Christianity, but who have in fact rejected a pale imitation of the real thing. There must also be a great many Christians who have lost sight of the basics. I want to look now at Mark chapter 8 in order to consider afresh those Christian basics. In this chapter, we see Jesus explaining that a Christian is someone who knows who Jesus is, understands why he came, and is prepared to follow him – whatever the cost. To some extent, looking at Mark chapter 8 will sum up what we've explored so far.

Who is Jesus?

This question has dominated the book of Mark up to chapter 8 and we, the readers, already know the answer. As we've seen, Mark's given the game away in the very first verse, where he tells us that this is a book of good news about Jesus Christ, the Son of God. It's a bit like an Agatha Christie novel beginning with the words, 'The butler did it.' You might think it would drain the book of all interest, but the fact is *that the disciples don't know what we know.* And we follow them around, watching as they try to make sense of Jesus. Jesus, for his part, forces them to ask questions about who he is by doing amazing things, as we've seen. They watch him calming a vicious storm, curing incurable illness, bringing a little girl back from the dead. They even hear him claiming to be able to forgive sin. And yet they don't draw the obvious conclusion: that this is God's Anointed One, the Christ, the Son of God, the one who'd been promised throughout the Bible. They were expecting it, were desperately hoping for it, but now that he's there, standing right in front of them, they just don't see it.

Have you ever seen one of those 'magic' pictures that seem to show one thing but – looked at another way – show something entirely different? The most well known of these images is probably the picture of a beautiful young woman that can also look like a hideous old hag. I have to admit that, despite staring at that picture for a long time, it was ages before I could see the beautiful young woman. All I saw was the hideous old hag. And if you're an amateur psychologist, I'm sure you could have some fun with that fact.

Well, in a similar way, Jesus also had two faces: the

human and the divine. The two were obvious, they were there for all to see, but even though the disciples stared and stared for several years, all they could see was the man. They couldn't see the divine face of Christ. Again and again, Mark draws our attention to their blindness. He does this, for example, in chapter 8 verses 17 and 18. Jesus is exasperated with them: *'Do you still not see or understand? Are your hearts hardened? Do you have eyes but fail to see, and ears but fail to hear?'* And then, quite strikingly, the next incident we read about is Jesus enabling a blind man to see. The miracle is quite unique. It's the only one of Jesus' miracles that happens *gradually*. First, Jesus touches the blind man, and he begins to see, but only vaguely. Then, he touches him again, and this time the man sees perfectly. Mark intends us to see this as a parallel to the gradual opening of the disciples' eyes. Of course, the disciples aren't physically blind; they are *spiritually* blind. And only Jesus can heal them.

Then, in verses 27 to 29, we see Jesus beginning to heal their spiritual blindness. The disciples won't be fully cured until later, when they understand what Jesus came to do and what it means to follow him. But here, for the first time, there is an indication that they know *who* Jesus is:

> Jesus and his disciples went on to the villages around Caesarea Philippi. On the way he asked them, 'Who do people say I am?'

That's a fairly safe question. It's a starter for ten. It's general knowledge, a bit like me asking you, 'Who won the last election?'.

> They replied, 'Some say John the Baptist; others say Elijah; and still others, one of the prophets.'

Fair enough. They're quite right to say that most people think that Jesus is – at the very least – on a par with the great prophets of the Bible, people like Elijah. But now Jesus asks a more uncomfortable question:

'But what about you?' he asked. 'Who do you say I am?'

There's a big difference between me asking you 'Who won the last election?' and me asking you, 'How did *you* vote in that election?' It's a personal question, and the answer tells me something about you. Jesus' question is a pivotal moment in Mark's Gospel, a moment in which Mark asks his readers to answer the same question: *Who do you say Jesus is?*

Peter answered, 'You are the Christ.'

This word 'Christ' has big implications. It means 'God's Anointed One'; it's a title of supreme authority, like 'King'. Peter is saying that Jesus is the ultimate King, the one promised in the Bible, the one who would rescue all those who trusted in him.

I wonder if we've seen that as we've looked at Jesus in Mark. Do we see the human face, or the divine face? At this point in his Gospel, Mark hopes we can see both. Yes, Jesus is a human being – but he is also God's great King, the Christ, the Son of God.

But it's not enough simply to know Jesus' true identity. You see, Peter gets the question of Jesus' identity absolutely right here. But when it comes to the question of what Jesus came to do, Peter gets it horribly wrong.

What did Jesus come to do?
If Jesus wants everyone to know who he truly is, why on

earth does he tell the disciples in Mark chapter 8 verse 30 'not to tell anyone about him'? It's because, as we're about to see in verses 31 to 33, Jesus knows that the disciples still have some learning to do before they can start telling people about him. Peter is right to identify Jesus as 'the Christ', but his actions in these verses reveal that he doesn't yet understand what the Christ came to do:

> He [Jesus] then began to teach them that the Son of Man must suffer many things and be rejected by the elders, chief priests and teachers of the law, and that he must be killed and after three days rise again. He spoke plainly about this, and Peter took him aside and began to rebuke him.

Mark here uses the words 'He then began to teach...' to introduce ideas about the Christ that we haven't read about before. So the disciples are being taught startling new things here. Jesus teaches them that the Son of Man (or 'Christ', to use Peter's title) must suffer, be rejected by the religious authorities, die, and after three days rise again. *That's* what he has come to do. The Bible predicted it, and Jesus knew perfectly well that the only way by which rebels could be brought back into a relationship with God was for him to die.

But Peter has this image of Jesus as King so clearly in his mind that it seems entirely inappropriate to him that Jesus would have to die. And he tells Jesus so. He takes him aside and gives him a pep talk. How on earth can a king bring in his kingdom by *dying*? That's ridiculous. But Jesus tells Peter he's got it all wrong:

> 'You do not have in mind the things of God, but the things of men.'

In a way, I don't blame Peter for thinking like this. After

all, there are two ways of looking at the cross. If, as Jesus says, we have in mind 'the things of men', there is tremendous weakness at the cross. Jesus seems exposed, humiliated and defeated. In Matthew's Gospel, passers-by shout up at him, 'Come down from the cross, if you are the Son of God!' From the human point of view, the cross seems to prove conclusively that Jesus was wrong. He was right about so many things, but if he really *was* the Son of God, why couldn't he come down from the cross? A king should be on a throne, not on a cross.

But Jesus responds to those who have in mind 'the things of men'. In chapter 26 of Matthew, verses 52 to 54, one of the disciples tries to resist the crowd that has come to arrest Jesus and kill him. We know from John's Gospel that the disciple is none other than Peter. He reaches for his sword and cuts off the ear of the high priest's servant.

> 'Put your sword back in its place,' Jesus said to him, 'for all who draw the sword will die by the sword. Do you think I cannot call on my Father, and he will at once put at my disposal more than twelve legions of angels? But how then would the Scriptures be fulfilled that say it must happen in this way?'

A Roman legion was made up of 6,000 soldiers, so what Jesus is saying here is that he has overwhelming power at his disposal. These angels could immediately come and attend to his needs as they do earlier in Mark. *But he chooses not to use this power.* Why? Because if he did so, 'how then would the Scriptures be fulfilled that say it must happen in this way?' Even here, as he pulls a sword to keep Jesus from being arrested, Peter has in mind 'the things of men'. He is still looking at the situation from a human perspective.

But what do we see if we look at the cross from another angle, from God's perspective? What do we see if we have in mind, as Jesus says, 'the things of God'? Then we can see the cross as part of God's rescue plan. We can see that Jesus *chooses* not to resist arrest, and that he *chooses* to be separated from God so that we don't have to be, paying the terrible price for our sin, being executed – in our place – for crimes he never committed. From God's perspective (and from ours if we have in mind the things of God), this is not weakness. In fact, there has never been a more powerful moment in history.

On 13 January 1982, millions of television viewers watched as a balding, middle-aged man swam in the icy-cold water of a river in Washington DC. Seven inches of snow had fallen that day. The water was so cold that the life expectancy of anyone in it was no more than a few minutes. A helicopter quickly reached the scene and let down a rope to haul the man to safety. The viewers at home were amazed as the man grabbed hold of the rope twice, then quite deliberately let it go. Each time the rope was lowered to him, he had a chance of survival – but he chose to let it go. And – in front of millions of mesmerized viewers – the man eventually died. It seems like a futile and pointless death. But we need to see the broader picture.

Five minutes earlier, at four o'clock p.m., Air Florida flight 90, a Boeing 737 jetliner carrying 83 passengers and crew, departed from National Airport's main runway. However, the ice that had built up on the wings as it waited for take-off prevented it from gaining sufficient altitude.

Traffic on the nearby 14th Street Bridge was heavy with commuters. *The Washington Post* newspaper described what happened next:

> With an awful metallic crack, a blue-and-white jet swept out of
> the swirling snow… smacked against one of the bridge's spans,
> sheared through five cars like a machete, ripped through 50
> feet of guard rail and plunged nose first into the frozen
> Potomac River.

The survivors struggled in the freezing river amid ice
chunks, debris, luggage, seat cushions and jet fuel. A
rescue helicopter arrived. Life vests were dropped, then a
flotation ball. The television cameras picked out a
balding, middle-aged man, passing them on to the others.
The helicopter then let down its rope. The man, who was
a strong swimmer, swam as fast as he could to the rope,
grabbed it, and gave it to somebody else who was then
pulled to safety. This happened twice before – exhausted
– the man drowned. When we have all the details in front
of us, an apparently futile death is shown to be
purposeful, daring and amazingly loving.

There are two ways of seeing the cross. We can see it
from a human perspective, as a pathetic and needless
death. Or we can see it from God's perspective, as our
only means of rescue. Our lives, as well as our deaths, will
be determined by the way in which we respond to what
Jesus did on the cross.

What does Jesus demand?

Return with me to Mark chapter 8 verses 34 to 37. Jesus
has just rebuked Peter for having in mind 'the things of
men'. He now calls the crowd to him and tells them what
it means to follow him. So if you want to know what it
means to be a Christian, these verses are addressed to you:

Then he called the crowd to him along with his disciples and said: 'If anyone would come after me, he must deny himself and take up his cross and follow me. For whoever wants to save his life will lose it, but whoever loses his life for me and for the gospel will save it. What good is it for a man to gain the whole world, yet forfeit his soul? Or what can a man give in exchange for his soul?'

According to Jesus' words here, following him means *a change of allegiance* and *a call to die*. Then, because these things are not easy, he goes on to give us *a convincing reason* for following him.

A change of allegiance

'If anyone would come after me, he must deny himself... and follow me.' Denying self is not about giving up chocolate for Lent (thankfully). But it's certainly no easier than that: it means turning away from our allegiance to ourselves and following him instead. It's a brief instruction, just half a verse, but it identifies our fundamental problem: we are essentially self-serving creatures. Our instinct is always towards self-preservation and self-promotion. That's why the cross, with its *lack* of these qualities, seems so unfathomable to us.

Who has the right to tell you how to live your life? Your gut response is probably the same as mine: no one does. Who has the right to tell you how you should spend your time? How to conduct your relationships? How to do your job? Surely our instinctive response is to cry, 'No one!' No one has the right to tell me how to live my life except me. But we're mistaken. God made us, he sustains us and we are dependent upon him for everything we have, so it is absurd (not to mention dangerous) to live in God's world as if we are independent of him. If you have young children who are still dependent upon you, don't you care how they live their lives? If you love them, you will seek to protect them from what you know will harm them. And that's God's attitude, too. But we push him away like spoiled children and make ourselves the ultimate authority.

So, first of all, Jesus tells us that we need to turn our backs on that selfish way of relating to God. He calls us in Mark chapter 1 to 'repent and believe the good news'. The word repent literally means 'to change one's direction'. To 'repent and believe' means I stop going my own way and instead say, 'Lord Jesus, I recognize who you are, and from now on I will allow you to take charge.' Turning away from our selfish instincts is hard, and it's an ongoing battle. Jesus warns us that this battle is all the more difficult because the devil opposes God and all those who are trying to follow him.

For many, the devil is a joke: the man in the red tights with the unconvincing horns and the plastic pitchfork. That's not the picture we're given in the Bible. In fact, you might have a hard time recognizing him if all you had to go on was the dubious mannequin they put up in shop windows at Halloween. But Jesus teaches that the devil's opposition is serious: even when people are listening to God's word being taught, the devil is at work. Jesus points this out in Luke chapter 8 verses 4 to 12, making it plain that people can hear God's words, but then find that 'the devil comes and takes away the word from their hearts, so that they may not believe and be saved'. Personally, I think it would be great if the devil started spitting and screaming if you got him anywhere near a church, as he does in films. At least he'd be easy to spot. But he's subtler than that. He wants God's word to fall on deaf ears – so don't expect to be immune from the devil's distractions just because you're in a church. He fights not only with subtlety and formidable perceptiveness, he also fights without moral principle or code of honour. You cannot appeal to the Geneva Convention or to Queensbury Rules where the devil is concerned.

Having said all that, let me also say that to ascribe every single mishap, inconvenience or unpleasantness to the devil is unwise. I've heard someone claim that just because they couldn't find a parking space at Sainsbury's, 'the devil must've really wanted to keep me away from the shops' (presumably because there was an urgent need for quiche at the church fête). It is dangerous to underestimate the devil's power, but it can be equally damaging to overestimate it. The Bible says that – thanks to the cross – the devil has already been defeated, and he knows 'that his time is short.'[1]

So changing our allegiance will not be easy, and it's something we need to do deliberately every day. But if you're sure that Jesus is God, then what he's asking for here is not inappropriate. He is asking that you give your life: the life he created, the life he daily sustains, the life he died to rescue. Indeed, when you see his goodness, selflessness and love, it becomes much easier to allow him to be Lord of your life: here is somebody who – judging by his life – will not let you down, and has your best interests at heart.

You may have noticed that there's an additional ingredient to Jesus' command:

---

[1] Revelation chapter 12 verse 12

'If anyone would come after me, he must deny himself and take up his cross and follow me.'

Not only must we deny ourselves if we are to follow him, we must also *take up our cross*.

A call to die

Remember where Jesus himself is going at this point. He is heading for the cross, as he has just told the disciples. Now Jesus warns potential followers that if they are to follow him, they too must head for the cross. Although it's unlikely that any of us will face a literal cross, the command is still a chilling one. Jesus is telling us here that if we commit ourselves to him, it will mean a martyrdom of one kind or another.

Now, I don't know what you were up to on *your* seventeenth birthday, but in 54 AD, Nero became the head of the most powerful empire on the planet, the Roman Empire. In effect, he became ruler of the world. Now, this wasn't an ideal state of affairs. At seventeen, you can be a bit impetuous. And whereas most of us were stacking shelves of a Saturday morning, Nero was indulging his lust for power by murdering anyone he thought was against him. As Nero's reign continued, his venom increasingly turned against Christians.

In 64 AD, a fire destroyed half the city of Rome and rumours spread that Nero (who wanted Rome cleared to make room for a massive building project) was responsible. Nero, sensing that public opinion was turning against him, passed the blame onto the Christians. He claimed that they had brought a curse on the city because they wouldn't worship the Roman gods. As a result, people who insisted on their allegiance to Christ were arrested, imprisoned and executed, often by being thrown to wild animals.

I became a Christian when I was sixteen, and although I never found myself being served to a lion, I nevertheless faced opposition. For example, I discovered that no matter which rugby team I played for, or which rugby club I was a member of, I became something of an outsider. That's not to say that I didn't really like the company or the rugby – far from it – but sometimes, especially on tours, I found myself alone. I found myself marginalized, more isolated than I was ever used to in those situations, and it was simply because I followed Christ. As Jesus himself said in John chapter 15 verses 18 to 20:

> 'If the world hates you, keep in mind that it hated me first. If you belonged to the world, it would love you as its own. As it is, you do not belong to the world, but I have chosen you out of the world. That is why the world hates you. Remember the words I spoke to you: "No servant is greater than his master." If they persecuted me, they will persecute you also.'

My suffering has been relatively mild. But it can be extremely distressing to find yourself attacked – even if only verbally – by those closest to you. If you follow Christ, there will be times when to do so will mean deliberately risking the anger and scorn of those you love most dearly. Jesus himself found that those who thought they knew him best – those he had grown up with – resented the claims he made. We read in chapter 6 of Mark that they 'took offence at him'. Elsewhere, as in Mark chapter 3, even Jesus' own family members think that he is 'out of his mind' for speaking and behaving as he does.

In the early years of the twentieth century, the polar explorer Ernest Shackleton put an advertisement in various London newspapers. He wanted to find men who would come with him on his expeditions. The advertisements said this: 'Men wanted for a hazardous journey. Small wages, bitter cold, long months in complete darkness, constant danger, safe return doubtful.' Funnily enough, there weren't many applicants.

But Christ's appeal in Mark chapter 8 is similar: 'Come and die. I'll die for you, but you must be prepared to die for me.' Those are the conditions if we are to follow him. Jesus, referring to some who initially respond with enthusiasm to the gospel, warns in Mark chapter 4 verses 16 and 17 that nevertheless, 'when trouble or persecution comes because of the word, they quickly fall away'. Note that Jesus uses the word 'when', not 'if'. Jesus expects trouble and persecution to come as a result of obedience to him, and so must his followers. There's no side door or VIP guest list; it's the same for everybody. And we don't hear much about that today, do we? We've managed to make Christianity safe. It's been tamed, made bland and cosy. But the Christians of 64 AD wouldn't have recognized it as Christianity. No, they understood that following Christ meant taking up your cross, and Jesus' instructions have not changed since then.

Let me stop here and make one thing very clear, in case it isn't already: *99.9% of the blessings of the Christian life are in the world to come.* And if you think that sounds like an exaggeration, see if you still feel the same way in a thousand years or ten thousand years. Don't get me wrong.

I love the Christian life. It is a life of great purpose, and it is a deep joy to know Christ and his forgiveness. But with Jesus' call for a change of allegiance, there is a call to die. If you've grasped what that means, you will want to think very seriously before committing your life to Christ. There seems an awful lot to lose. With that in mind, Jesus goes on to give us a convincing reason for switching our allegiance to him.

A convincing reason
If we think about following Christ in purely earthly terms, the cost seems too high. So Jesus' aim in verses 35 to 37 of Mark chapter 8 is to give us the right perspective:

> 'For whoever wants to save his life will lose it, but whoever loses his life for me and for the gospel will save it. What good is it for a man to gain the whole world, yet forfeit his soul? Or what can a man give in exchange for his soul?'

This passage insists that our 'souls' are the most precious thing we have. If we lose our soul, there is *nothing* we can do to get it back. So here Jesus wants to lift our eyes from the present and fix them on the future. And the Bible says that the future is vitally important, because it's eternal. When we die, it's not the end. Jesus teaches us here that there is a connection between how we live now, and what will happen after death. As Maximus says in the film *Gladiator*: 'What we do in life echoes in eternity.'

And there's a twist, because those who try to save their lives will lose them, while those prepared to lose their lives will gain them. Jesus knows very well how much we want to cling on to our lives, to do what *we* want to do when *we* want to do it. But he warns us that if we live in that way, we'll ultimately lose the very thing we are so desperate to cling onto. He tells us that if we really want to hold onto our lives, there's only one option open to us: we must allow him to take control.

Many people think that they have too much to lose by doing this. But those who do let Jesus take control actually discover for themselves an exhilarating freedom and joy they never dreamed existed. As Jesus himself promises in John chapter 8 verses 31 to 32:

'If you hold to my teaching, you are really my disciples. Then you will know the truth, and the truth will set you free.'

In addition, God never makes demands of us without supplying the means to meet them, and we will look at what those means are in the final section of this book, 'Further Exploration'.

Moreover, whatever we might lose by following Christ pales when we consider heaven. For example, Revelation chapter 21 verse 4 gives a privileged glimpse of what heaven will be like:

There will be no more death or mourning or crying or pain, for the old order of things has passed away.

In other words, we won't have to put up with sin any more. At last, we will be free to enjoy all of the good things that God provides – eternally. Indeed, as it says in Revelation, God himself will wipe every tear from our eyes. There will be no more regret, no more unfulfilled dreams, no more lost loved ones, no more fear, no more bitterness, no more broken hearts, no more loneliness, no more 'religiosity', *no more sin*. And the Bible affirms that heaven is not a place where individuality is lost. Far from it.

It's a place where all our potential as individuals is finally fulfilled. This is not a pipe dream, or a cruel mirage, but an amazing reality earned for us by Christ's death, and proved by Christ's resurrection.

As we learned in the last chapter, Christ will judge the world – whether we like it or not. We can choose whether or not this judge will also be our saviour. And, ultimately, we will be treated very fairly. Christ will treat us in exactly the same way as we have treated him, as he tells us in Mark chapter 8 verse 38:

> 'If anyone is ashamed of me and my words in this adulterous and sinful generation, the Son of Man will be ashamed of him when he comes in his Father's glory with the holy angels.'

Because Christ is the person who will judge the world, it is therefore not a suicidal gesture to entrust him with my life. By doing so I know that my life will be saved. Jesus pleads with us to give up the very things that will destroy us – self-love, self-worship, self-will – and pleads with us not to waste our souls.

In 1000 AD, 186 years after the death of Emperor Charlemagne, officials of the Emperor Otto reopened Charlemagne's tomb. Before them was an extraordinary sight. In the midst of all the finery buried with him – the gold, the jewels, the priceless treasure – there was the skeleton of Charlemagne himself, still seated on his throne, still wearing his crown. In his lap there lay a Bible, and a bony finger rested on Mark chapter 8 verse 36: 'What good is it for a man to gain the whole world, yet forfeit his soul?' I wonder what answer the Emperor gave.

08

Choices – King Herod

What is it that determines the choices we make? Is it our consciences? I only ask because my conscience is currently being pricked by a one-year subscription to a magazine called *Men's Health,* and in the May edition it promised that I could have a flat belly by summer.

Well, it's summer, and I don't. But I'd love to. It'd be great to have 'rock-hard abs' where at present I have something that looks like a family-size pack of marshmallows. (It's the old gag: 'I now have a furniture problem: my chest is in my drawers.' Hilarious.) But, to be honest, I'd rather try liposuction than actually do the exercises that *Men's Health* suggests. I never before realized the complete truth of what Meryl Streep's character says in The Bridges of Madison County: 'We are the choices we have made.'

Men's Health doesn't have many articles on developing a healthy conscience, much less on actually listening to one. They know that most of their readers think of conscience as an imposition on their lives. Conscience is a bore. It asks people to act in ways that inconvenience them. It either stops people from doing things they'd otherwise enjoy, or it takes away their enjoyment when they ignore their conscience and do the thing anyway. Conscience is a nag, it never shuts up, it will not leave us in peace to live in the way we want to.

And yet, if I'd listened to my conscience during the month of May, I'd now be – according to *Men's Health* anyway – a 'leaning tower of power', as opposed to a wobbling vat of fat. Not only that, but listening to my conscience – and by that I mean the God-given sense of what is right and what is wrong – will affect far more than my body. *It will affect the ultimate destiny of my soul.* Why? Because 'we are the choices we have made'.

Herod chose to rebel

This isn't Herod the Great, the man who murdered all the baby boys living in the region where Jesus was born. No, that Herod died almost immediately after the massacre. The Herod we are going to look at now was his son, Herod Antipas, who was ruler of Galilee.

By the time we hear about him in Mark chapter 6, he has been married for over 20 years to the daughter of a king who lives in a neighbouring area. While visiting his brother Philip, however, he falls in love with his brother's wife, Herodias. He proposes to her, and she accepts on the condition that he gets rid of his present wife. He agrees. Herod chose to rebel against God's law. Does he *know* he's rebelling? Yes, because a man that he knows is 'righteous and holy' – John the Baptist – has been bravely telling King Herod that 'it is not lawful for you to have your brother's wife'.

John the Baptist is a man we read about right at the beginning of Mark, a friendless, solitary figure, teaching 'repentance for the forgiveness of sins'. And yet this humble man, armed only with God's word, disturbs King Herod greatly:

> When Herod heard John, he was greatly puzzled; yet he liked
> to listen to him.

Mark tells us that Herod was 'greatly puzzled'. This doesn't mean that John's teaching confused him; it means that his *morals* were thrown into confusion. John's words greatly troubled him. Why? Because John exposed his rebellion against God. Herod knew he should turn from his adultery, but he would not. Perhaps you have experienced similar discomfort as you've come to realize that you've been living your life for yourself, without reference to the one who made you. Perhaps, like Herod listening to John, you see the godliness of Jesus and want to go on listening to Jesus' words, despite the disturbance they may cause.

Herod puts John in prison, perhaps in part to protect him from his wife Herodias, who wants John dead because of what he has been preaching.

> So Herodias nursed a grudge against John and wanted to kill
> him. But she was not able to, because Herod feared John and
> protected him...

So Herod continues to listen to John, even though John's words disturb him.

Day after day it goes on. The people at the palace must have thought that their king had gone religious, listening to this strange figure preach as he did. 'Herod feared John' to the extent that he even 'protected him', but there was nevertheless something that Herod was not prepared to do.

Herod chose not to repent
Yes, he would listen. Yes, he acknowledged that John was

a just and holy man. Yes, he was even prepared to protect John. *But he would not stop his adultery*. He would not turn away from what he knew was wrong. In other words, he would not repent.

Then one day, on his birthday, he gives a banquet for all his high officials, his military commanders and the leading men of Galilee. Notice how Mark describes the occasion: 'Finally the opportune time came.' It's an opportune time for both Herod and for his wife, Herodias. For her, it is an opportunity to finally kill John. For him, it is an opportunity to finally, and publicly, repent of his wrongdoing. Notice who seizes the opportunity – and who misses it.

During the banquet, Herodias's daughter Salome performs a dance which 'pleased' Herod and his dinner guests. Put literally, she does a lascivious dance that gets the half-drunk guests sexually aroused. Herod, in a phrase designed to impress upon his guests what a liberal, generous man he is, says to this teenage girl:

> 'Ask me for anything you want, and I'll give it to you.' And he promised her with an oath, 'Whatever you ask I will give you, up to half my kingdom.'

As he said it, all his friends and officials were probably laughing and clapping him on the back. The girl runs to her mother and asks her what she should ask Herod for. Herodias doesn't need to be asked twice:

> 'The head of John the Baptist.'

Back the girl runs to Herod: 'I want you to give me right now the head of John the Baptist on a platter.'

Herod is suddenly the only one not laughing in the

banqueting hall. His bravado sinks within him as he hears this young girl utter those shocking words.

And this is the key moment in Herod's life. He is suddenly in an extremely dangerous place. If 'we are the choices we have made', then this choice will have a profound effect on what Herod will become. And it's a terribly hard choice to make, what with all the oaths he's made, and the guests he's trying to impress. But there it is. Either he says, 'Look, I shouldn't have made the oaths I made – it was a stupid thing to do. I can't kill John. He's a good man. I know the things he's said have been hard to accept, but he's always spoken the truth. I will not kill him.' Or, alternatively, he caves in to the fierce pressure of those around him, gamely pretending to laugh with all his guests, and suppressing his conscience once more.

What will he choose?

> The king was greatly distressed, but because of his oaths and his dinner guests, he did not want to refuse her. So he immediately sent an executioner with orders to bring John's head. The man went, beheaded John in the prison, and brought back his head on a platter. He presented it to the girl, and she gave it to her mother.

Much as he feared John, he feared his guests more. And when all is said and done, I wonder if Herod's guests really *did* respect him any the more for keeping his drunken oaths and needlessly slaughtering a man he had previously protected.

But how many of us would have done something similar in Herod's position? The fact remains that many, many people will do just that: in the moment of decision, they will deny what they know is right because of what the family will think, because of what business colleagues may do, or because of what friends will say. Or because they know it will mean changing much-loved habits.

Mark's account suggests a comparison of John with Jesus. Both preached the same gospel: that we need to turn from our rebellion against God, and accept the rescue he has lovingly provided. Both were protected by powerful men – Herod and Pontius Pilate – men who both tried to remain neutral but could not. And both John and Jesus suffered violent deaths as a result. There is, of course, one further point of comparison. Why were both John and Jesus killed? Because in both cases people would not *repent*.

What choices will we make? It's an important question because, although we are free to repent or not to repent, we are not free to determine the consequences of our actions. Herod's story is horrific – not just because of the gory details, but because it shows that for those who repeatedly choose not to repent, it becomes increasingly less likely that they will ever do so. In Mark chapters 1 to 3, we see Jesus' awesome power and authority. In chapters 4 to 5, we see the power of his teaching and of his word. And yet, at the beginning of chapter 6, we see him rejected by his *home town*. Their familiarity with Jesus bred contempt, they take offence at him, and they reject him. Jesus' response in subsequent chapters is to take his preaching elsewhere. He instructs his disciples to do likewise, saying that if people will not listen, they should move on. That's the pattern: the message will be rejected by some, who will themselves be rejected because of their response.

Herod is mentioned a final time in the Gospels, in

Luke chapter 23. Luke records that Pontius Pilate sends Jesus to Herod when he learns that Jesus is from the area Herod controls. The meeting is ominous – not because of what is said, but rather because of what is *not* said:

> When Herod saw Jesus, he was greatly pleased, because for a long time he had been wanting to see him. From what he had heard about him, he hoped to see him perform some miracle. He plied him with many questions, but Jesus gave him no answer.

You see, there comes a time when, after repeatedly refusing to repent, there is no longer an opportunity to do so. It is easy to put it off, to say that we don't have the time, to think that we have too much to lose, but Herod's story reminds us that we may not get an opportunity later.

When Herod gets no answer from Jesus, he and his soldiers mock him by dressing Jesus in an elegant robe and sending him back to Pilate, who enjoys the joke. We read that on that day, 'Herod and Pilate became friends – before this they had been enemies.' This should be a warning to us: rejecting Jesus' call to repent and believe may earn us the approval of other people, but it will eventually earn us the rejection of Jesus.

09

Choices – James, John and Bartimaeus

Value this time in your life, kids, because this is the time in your life when you still have your choices, and it goes by so quickly. When you're a teenager you think you can do anything, and you do. Your twenties are a blur. Your thirties, you raise your family, you make a little money and you think to yourself, 'What happened to my twenties?' Your forties, you grow a little pot belly, you grow another chin. The music starts to get too loud and one of your old girlfriends from high school becomes a grandmother. Your fifties, you have a minor surgery. You'll call it a procedure, but it's a surgery. Your sixties, you have a major surgery, the music is still loud but it doesn't matter because you can't hear it anyway. Seventies, you and the wife retire to Fort Lauderdale, you start eating dinner at two, lunch around ten, breakfast the night before. And you spend most of your time wandering around malls looking for the ultimate in soft yogurt and muttering, 'how come the kids don't call?' By your eighties, you've had a major stroke, and you end up babbling to some Jamaican nurse who your wife can't stand but who you call mama. Any questions?

This is Mitch Robbins in the film *City Slickers* offering his young children a little too much information. But when we have difficult choices ahead of us, that's exactly what we need to make the right decision: we need to know the hard facts.

We're going to look now finally at Mark chapter 10. Jesus has already told his disciples that he must be rejected by the religious authorities and killed. Jesus then begins leading them to Jerusalem. The disciples are astonished, and those following Jesus are afraid. Why? Because the religious authorities – those who will have him killed – *are based in Jerusalem*. He is marching determinedly into the jaws of death. In case any of them have missed the point, he repeats it for them:

> 'We are going up to Jerusalem,' he said, 'and the Son of Man will be betrayed to the chief priests and teachers of the law. They will condemn him to death and will hand him over to the Gentiles, who will mock him and spit on him, flog him and kill him. Three days later he will rise.'

By 'Gentiles', Jesus means the Roman authorities. Jesus Christ, God's King in God's world, will be condemned in the capital city by the nation's leaders.

Against that backdrop, two of his disciples – James and John – make a request that is breathtakingly inappropriate.

James and John

Although they call Jesus their 'teacher', how much have they really understood?

> Then James and John, the sons of Zebedee, came to him. 'Teacher,' they said, 'we want you to do for us whatever we ask.'
>
> 'What do you want me to do for you?' he asked.
>
> They replied, 'Let one of us sit at your right and the other at your left in your glory.'

Jesus has just told them that he is deliberately heading for Jerusalem, even though he knows that he will suffer and die there. But suffering and death don't figure in the thinking of James and John. They reckon that when Jesus' kingdom is established, there will be an unholy scramble for the best seats, so naturally they think it would be sensible to get in first and make an advance reservation. They are measuring their lives in terms of human achievement and status. Many people want the best job, the best car, the best house, the best seats at the theatre – and these two followers of Jesus are no different. Not only do they seek prestige, but they want power too: 'Let one of us sit at your right and the other at your left in your glory.' The implication is of sitting on thrones, with the power to summon and dismiss as they see fit. They obviously still haven't understood that Jesus – the person whose example they are supposed to be following – *must die.*

And if we have an eye for what is currently going on around us, we'll see that there is this lust for power and prestige almost everywhere. We certainly see it in big business and industry. We can also see it in the medical profession, the legal profession, in sports and in the arts, and there's no doubt it infects the world of politics as well. And, of course, we see it in the church. It's easy to turn the pulpit into a throne of authority and power.

Jesus knows that James and John are missing the point, and takes them to task: 'You don't know what you are asking.' He beckons them, and us, along a different path:

'You know that those who are regarded as rulers of the Gentiles lord it over them, and their high officials exercise authority over them. Not so with you.'

Those four words should be underlined in every Bible: *Not so with you*. Jesus is saying that those who wish to follow him must act in the opposite way to the world, where the 'high officials' exercise authority over the 'rulers', who in turn like to 'lord it' over those beneath them. James and John – like all of Christ's followers since – are not to embark on this kind of power trip, but instead follow the example their King sets.

> 'For even the Son of Man did not come to be served, but to serve, and to give his life as a ransom for many.'

Unlike earthly rulers, Jesus uses his power *to serve*. This is the big contrast between James and John and Jesus. The last thing on the minds of James and John when they make their request of Jesus is *service*. They want nothing more than *to be served*, and what's worse, to be served by the very man who will save their lives.

By contrast, Jesus goes the way of the cross. He doesn't seek his own honour, but instead, in his concern for others, he walks deliberately towards pain and humiliation. The difference between what the disciples choose to ask for and the way in which their master lives is dramatic. They choose to ask for glory, Jesus wants to serve. The symbol of Christianity is a cross rather than a throne, a crown of thorns rather than a crown of gold. We're used to imagining worldly leadership as a pyramid, with those at the top governing all those underneath. But Jesus turns that upside down:

> 'Instead, whoever wants to become great among you must be your servant, and whoever wants to be first must be slave of all.'

The disciples have yet to grasp the truth which Jesus knows full well as he heads towards Jerusalem: that the only way to be great in God's kingdom is to humble oneself. To serve rather than be served. And if that is true for Jesus – a man with God's authority and God's power – it will certainly be true for us.

But James and John aren't the only ones in this chapter who make a request of Jesus.

Bartimaeus

> As Jesus and his disciples, together with a large crowd, were leaving the city, a blind man, Bartimaeus (that is, the Son of Timaeus), was sitting by the roadside begging. When he heard that it was Jesus of Nazareth, he began to shout, 'Jesus, Son of David, have mercy on me!'

Bartimaeus is different from the disciples in many ways. Apart from the fact of his physical blindness, he is a beggar who has nothing of material value. He calls Jesus 'the Son of David' – in other words, God's King in God's world. It's the only place in Mark that we see someone recognize Jesus in this way.

Notice, too, that while the disciples want Jesus to do whatever they ask of him, Bartimaeus begs for mercy:

> Many rebuked him and told him to be quiet, but he shouted all the more, 'Son of David, have mercy on me!'

The crowd obviously thinks that this beggar is unworthy of Jesus' attention, but Bartimaeus is desperate for his help. He knows he deserves nothing from Jesus, and so cries out for mercy.

> Jesus stopped and said, 'Call him.'
>
> So they called to the blind man, 'Cheer up! On your feet! He's calling you.' Throwing his cloak aside, he jumped to his feet and came to Jesus.
>
> 'What do you want me to do for you?' Jesus asked him.
>
> The blind man said, 'Rabbi, I want to see.'

The disciples wanted thrones, glory, power and prestige, but this man asks simply 'to see'. That's one of the great ironies in this passage. After all, as we've seen, it's the disciples who are really blind. But this man, for all his physical limitations, has insight that far surpasses that of the disciples. He has seen who Jesus really is and what it means to follow him. Not only that, but he is painfully aware of his disability; James and John are unaware of theirs.

Jesus calls Bartimaeus to him and asks him exactly the same question that he asked the disciples: 'What do you want me to do for you?' But while James and John display vanity in the presence of Jesus, this man, conscious of his blindness, shows complete trust and dependence. And notice that while the disciples were reprimanded for their request, *Bartimaeus is healed*.

> 'Go,' said Jesus, 'your faith has healed you.' Immediately he received his sight and followed Jesus along the road.

James and John ask for status in God's kingdom and receive a sharp put-down, but Bartimaeus asks for *mercy*, and Jesus graciously responds.

If you are someone who has not yet put your trust in Jesus for the forgiveness of your sin, you need to learn that the right choice to make is to cry out for mercy, not chase after worldly recognition. The self-interest of James and John meant that they could see no reason for Jesus to die. Their self-centredness kept them from seeing that they needed to be rescued. And Jesus can't help those who don't see that they need him. By wonderful contrast, he freely welcomes those who understand their complete dependence upon him.

One last film quote, then. *Apt Pupil* is a film about a boy who discovers that an old man now living in his neighbourhood has a secret past. In fact, the man is a war criminal. It is a film about many things, not least the nature of evil. And as the film considers these issues, it ponders what it means to have the responsibility of choice:

> All of us have heard the story of Icarus, the young boy who took the wings his father built for him, wings that were meant to carry him over the ocean to freedom, and used them instead for a joyride. For a brief moment Icarus felt what it was like to live like a god, to touch the sun, to soar above the common man. And for doing so he paid the ultimate price. Like Icarus, we too have been given gifts: knowledge, education, experience. And with these gifts comes the responsibility of choice. We alone decide how our talents are bestowed upon the world. This is our destiny and we hold it in the palm of our hands.

Although God gave us the gifts we have, only we can choose how to use them. But there are consequences that will flow from that decision. Over to you.

If you've become convinced of who Jesus is and what he came to do, and you understand what it will mean to follow him, you might like to pray the following simple prayer. There's nothing magical about the words I've used – it's just a way of saying that you know you need to be rescued, and that you trust Jesus to be your rescuer:

Lord God, I have not loved you with all my heart, soul, mind and strength.

I am sorry for the way I've lived, rebelling against you in so many ways.

I now understand who Jesus is. I understand that when he died on the cross, he was being punished in my place, so that I could be forgiven and have eternal life. I gratefully accept that gracious gift.

From now on, please give me the desire to obey you, and help me live the Christian life, whatever the cost.

Don't worry if you feel no immediate change. Jesus promises that anyone who responds to his voice can be sure that their sins are forgiven: 'Here I am! I stand at the door and knock. If anyone hears my voice and opens the door, I will come in and eat with him, and he with me.'

You are about to explore an amazing new life.

Further Exploration

In a book this size, I haven't been able to explore every aspect of Christianity. But there are some things I'd like to mention here, particularly for the benefit of those who have just begun to trust Christ for themselves.

After all, as we saw in Chapter 7 ('What Is A Christian?'), it's not going to be easy. I mentioned there that God never makes demands of us without supplying the means to meet them, so now I'd like to look at four ways in which God provides for his people: prayer, the church, the Holy Spirit and the Bible.

Prayer

There's a tiny whitewashed church in a tumbleweed-strewn shanty town. Clint Eastwood rides into view and finds a cowering monk, dressed in a coarse brown robe and clutching his hands together prayerfully. He looks up at Clint with a mixture of expectation and cowardice. Our hero glares out at him from beneath his broad-brimmed hat. He's about to ride out and give the baddies a good kicking. 'Can I come with you?' asks the monk. 'Nope. It's dangerous, and you don't know how to use a gun.' 'But I really want to help!' And at this, Clint contemptuously spurs his horse into action and shouts back at him, 'Well, I guess you can always pray.'

This idea that prayer is a weak measure, employed by

people who can't do anything practical to help, is a popular one. The assumption is that God will not answer. It's like that episode of *The Simpsons*, where Homer says, 'Dear Lord, the gods have been good to me. As an offering, I present these milk and cookies. If you wish me to eat them instead, please give me no sign whatsoever. [Brief pause] Thy bidding will be done.' And he scoffs the lot. But for Christians, prayer is not ineffectual; it's extremely powerful. Not because of the person praying, but because of the person being prayed to.

Take – for example – the prayer the disciples pray in Acts chapter 4. They start their prayer like this:

> 'Sovereign Lord… you made the heaven and the earth and the sea, and everything in them.'

At this point, things could not be much worse for them. Their leader is no longer with them and their two main spokesmen have just been interrogated by the highest religious authorities, who are determined to shut them up. Rightly, in the face of such fierce opposition, they pray together, and it is interesting to see who they address their prayer to: 'Sovereign Lord'.

Indeed, their whole prayer goes on to remind us of how irresistibly powerful this Sovereign Lord is. They pray to the one who 'made the heaven and the earth and the sea, and everything in them'. So he made the world we live in and all the people who populate it. By quoting from Scripture written hundreds of years previously, they remind themselves that this 'Sovereign Lord' fully expects earthly powers to 'gather together' and plot against him and his 'Anointed One', but that this plotting is 'in vain'. They continue:

'Indeed Herod and Pontius Pilate met together with the Gentiles and the people of Israel in this city to conspire against your holy servant Jesus, whom you anointed.'

In effect, they remind themselves – and us – that although the situation *seems* to be terribly dangerous, the Sovereign Lord has seen it all coming a mile off. God is so completely in control, in fact, that 'They did what your power and will had decided beforehand should happen.' That is not to say that God's enemies are puppets who have no choice but to disobey God. The Bible makes it clear that everyone has the choice to obey or to disobey. But the disciples' prayer here gives us a glimpse of just how futile it is to oppose God: 'They did what your power and will had decided beforehand should happen.' You have to be unimaginably powerful to have your enemies do your bidding, even as they seek to destroy you. But that is precisely the kind of God who hears Jesus' followers when they pray.

So in the face of powerful opposition it is vital to pray, knowing that you are praying to a God who is more powerful. Romans chapter 8 tells us that 'in all things God works for the good of those who love him'. It's important to remember that our 'good' may not be what we expect or want. Rather than removing us from a particular situation, God may instead choose to equip us to handle it better. In the case of the disciples in Acts chapter 4, God acts in a very visible way. They ask for his help to 'speak your word with great boldness' in the face of the threats and opposition confronting them, and then we read of the result: 'After they prayed, the place where they were meeting was shaken. And they were all filled

with the Holy Spirit and spoke the word of God boldly.'
So firstly, when Christians pray they are talking to the
Sovereign Lord who always acts powerfully, even if not
always visibly.

But that's not all. As well as being 'Sovereign Lord',
God is also – if you're a Christian – *your* Father. In
Matthew chapter 6, Jesus teaches his followers specifically
how they should pray:

> 'This, then, is how you should pray: "Our Father in heaven,
> hallowed be your name..."'

Perhaps the most striking thing here is that Jesus tells his
followers to refer to God as 'Our Father'. This reflects the
intimacy people can have with God because of the cross.
Indeed, the word Jesus uses for 'Father' is closer to our
word 'Daddy'. To be on such intimate terms with God is a
tremendous privilege. It means that Christians can speak to
God as they might speak to a loving earthly father: to thank
him, ask him for support or forgiveness, confide in him,
pour out their hearts to him. And nothing is beyond his
concern, as we see in Philippians chapter 4 verse 6:

> Do not be anxious about anything, but in everything, by
> prayer and petition, with thanksgiving, present your requests
> to God.

Talking to a person this frankly and consistently deepens
our relationship with them, and indeed our love for them.
In the same way, Jesus teaches that prayer is one way in
which Christians deepen their relationship with their
Father. It also teaches them to be increasingly dependent
on God for all their needs. Of course, dependence on a
human being can be a bad thing. Unlike an earthly father,

however, God always has the power to do what is best for those who love him. As we've seen, nothing is beyond his control, or his concern.

Some people treat prayer like the fourth emergency service – after the police, the ambulance and the fire brigade. A crisis comes – be it an exam I'm under-prepared for, or a traffic jam when I'm late for a meeting – and I think to myself, well, there's nothing else for it, I'd better pray. But Jesus teaches that Christians shouldn't only call upon God when they're in trouble. Instead, they should pray constantly, just as he did.

Why should Christians pray all the time? Well, we've already seen that prayer teaches them dependence, deepens their relationship with God and allows them to call on God's power. But, in addition, Jesus teaches his followers that prayer enables them to resist temptation. Look at verse 38 of Mark chapter 14: 'Watch and pray so that you will not fall into temptation. The spirit is willing, but the body is weak.'

There were a couple of blokes in my rugby team who lived their lives without reference to God, but who nevertheless used to 'cross' themselves as they ran on to the field. It was a little self-help formula they used: a quick, superstitious prayer to get them in the right frame of mind. But that's not what Christian prayer is about. As we've seen, it is the privilege of constantly pouring out your heart to an all-powerful Father. Spike Milligan was asked if he ever prayed and he said, 'Yes, I do pray desperately all the time, but I've no idea who I'm praying to.' For Christians, this is no longer the case: they know exactly who they're praying to.

The church

'Never have I encountered such foul, mindless perversity!', says the baby-eating Bishop of Bath and Wells in *Blackadder II,* 'Have you considered a career in the church?' I know that church is not a popular subject. But let me get one thing clear straight away. When the Bible talks about 'the church', it's not referring to a building or to an old-fashioned institution. It's simply referring to all those who have put their trust in Christ. (It's a collective noun like 'a gaggle of geese'. Rather than forming a gaggle, Christians make up 'a church' – which is a bit more dignified, I think you'll agree.) And God intends Christians to be a support to one another.

Now, hang on to your hats, because I'm going to say something profound: *human beings are influenced by those they spend time with.* I don't suppose that comes as a surprise to you, but it is an easy truth to forget. And the Bible reminds Christians that the people they spend time with can have a positive or a negative influence on them. Spending time in the company of other people who are seeking to follow Christ is one of the ways in which God wants Christians to be encouraged and inspired. We read in Hebrews chapter 10:

> Let us not give up meeting together, as some are in the habit of doing, but let us encourage one another.

The writer knows that, without this mutual encouragement, it will be hard to persevere. So if you are a Christian, it's very important to find a church where the teaching is faithful to God's word, where the people you meet are eager to welcome and support you, and where you are able to serve others. Sadly, not every church you visit will do these things. So don't be afraid to keep looking until you find one that does.

Psalm 1 also reminds Christians that they will be influenced by those with whom they keep company:

> Blessed is the man who does not walk in the counsel of the wicked or stand in the way of sinners or sit in the seat of mockers.

Notice the way in which the psalmist describes what the blessed man is *not* like. This 'unblessed' man goes from walking, to standing, to sitting: he is gradually grinding to a halt. How does this happen? It begins simply by walking alongside 'the wicked', listening to their 'counsel', getting their advice and perspective on the world. If this carries on long enough, he'll begin to pick up their habits and attitudes for himself. Finally, he ends up sitting 'in the seat of mockers' – not only participating in this way of life, but actually mocking those who don't. Likewise, look at Proverbs chapter 13 verse 20:

> He who walks with the wise grows wise, but a companion of fools suffers harm.

For the Christian, this means – among other things – that they must spend time in the company of other Christians.

And because God has now become their 'Father', other Christians have become their brothers and sisters. Now you may be thinking, 'Hang on, I've already got a brother/sister, and one's enough.' But nevertheless, 1 Peter chapter 1 tells Christian brothers and sisters that they should 'love one another deeply, from the heart'. It's not easy to do this, of course. But when Christians remember that they've been forgiven so much themselves, they will be much more likely to forgive what is unlovable in others.

Even in the very early days of the church, the mark of authentic Christian living was the love that Christians showed one another:

> They walk in all humility and kindness, and falsehood is not found among them. They love one another. He that has distributes liberally to him that does not have. If they see a stranger they bring him under their own roof and rejoice over him as if he were their own brother. For they call themselves brothers not after the flesh but after the spirit.[1]

These are the words of a non-Christian observer in 125 AD. Even though he was not a believer himself, he could see the reality of what it meant to be a spiritual brother or sister because the whole Christian community – the church – expressed this love so powerfully.

God not only provides Christians with a new family for their support. He actually provides them with his Spirit.

The Holy Spirit

Consider this. At the end of Jesus' life here on earth, after a succession of awe-inspiring miracles and the most amazing teaching the world has ever heard, how many followers do you think Jesus had attracted to himself? According to Acts chapter 1 verse 15, about 120.

The surprising fact is that despite his remarkable life, very few people were following Christ at the end of his time here on earth. However, read on beyond the Gospels – to the book of Acts – and see what happens after Jesus leaves his disciples. For some reason, his influence becomes even more powerful and compelling *in his absence*. Nine

---

[1] Helen B. Harris, *The Newly Recovered Apology of Aristides: Its Doctrines and Ethics* (London: Hodder and Stoughton, 1891), pp. 106-7.

days after Jesus left them, even though opposition to his followers had become ever more violent, we read that in one day no fewer than *3,000 people* joined that tiny group of 120. After that, Acts tells us that more and more people were added to their number on a daily basis. Something sudden and extraordinary must have happened soon after Jesus left his followers. In fact, Jesus had already predicted it – and had told his disciples what they should expect once he'd gone. John chapter 16 verse 7:

> 'But I tell you the truth: It is for your good that I am going away. Unless I go away, the Counsellor will not come to you; but if I go, I will send him to you.'

It is this 'Counsellor' who is responsible for the tremendous growth of the early church.

Earlier, in John chapter 14, Jesus had already promised that the Counsellor – or 'Spirit' – would come to live 'in' those who follow him:

> 'If you love me, you will obey what I command. And I will ask the Father, and he will give you another Counsellor to be with you for ever – the Spirit of truth. The world cannot accept him, because it neither sees him nor knows him. But you know him, for he lives with you and will be in you. I will not leave you as orphans; I will come to you.'

It's a promise that still holds true today in the experience of every human being who begins following Christ: the Spirit will come to live 'with you' and 'in you'. In fact, the Greek word translated here as 'Counsellor' is *parakletos*, which described a pilot guiding a ship into port. It was also used to describe a friend comforting a bereaved person. Literally, the word means 'one who is called alongside'. Notice, too, that Jesus talks about *another* Counsellor. In effect, he is saying that this Spirit will do for believers what he himself has done for them while on earth: advising them, teaching them, guiding them and so on. Indeed, the Spirit who comes to live in Christians is the Spirit of Christ himself.

I could summarize quite simply what the Holy Spirit brings to the life of those who follow Christ: he brings *conflict*, but he also brings a supernatural *calm*. Let me explain what I mean. The conflict comes because the Spirit urges and empowers Christians to wage war against their sinful nature, as Galatians chapter 5 verses 16 to 17 makes clear:

> So I say, live by the Spirit, and you will not gratify the desires of the sinful nature. For the sinful nature desires what is contrary to the Spirit, and the Spirit what is contrary to the sinful nature. They are in conflict with each other, so that you do not do what you want.

In other words, although the Spirit makes Christians *want* to please God (in fact he makes them delight in doing so), the sinful nature continues to fight against that desire. This feeling of inner conflict is strangely comforting, however, because it confirms that the Spirit is real and at work.

So, there is conflict, but the Spirit also brings with him an unearthly *calm*. Boris Becker, the great German tennis player, once said:

> I'd won Wimbledon twice before, once as the youngest player. I was rich: I had all the material possessions I could want – money, cars, women – everything. I know this is a

> cliché. It's the old song of the movie and pop star who committed suicide; they had everything yet they are so unhappy. I had no inner peace.

The Bible says that the reason for Becker's lack of peace is separation from the God who made him. But when a person begins following Christ, they no longer feel that separation. Indeed, because the Spirit now resides in that person, God is with them forever. That presence provides peace, described in Philippians chapter 4 as 'the peace of God, which transcends all understanding'. Paul writes in Romans chapter 8 that this peace comes from a deep inner conviction that the follower of Christ is one of 'God's children', no longer separated from him, and certain to be with him in heaven. For Christians facing opposition, that assurance of eternal life is a very precious thing.

The Holy Spirit is powerful – powerful enough to actually change those who follow Christ. The first time I can remember the Spirit changing me in this way was when I was sixteen and had just become a Christian. Rugby was central to my life (now, of course, it's only very important indeed). My friend John had just got into the first team at school, and I was so jealous that I couldn't sleep. One day, after a practice in which John had played particularly well, my sense of jealousy and desperation was such that I walked into a shed beside the pitch, knelt down and said, 'Lord Jesus, please take this jealousy away.' I'd like to say that at that point another boy burst into the shed to tell me that John had been dropped, but no. Instead, I had a sense of being changed from within. Three weeks later (after John had in fact been dropped), he came up to me and thanked me for remaining on friendly terms with him when so many others had allowed their jealousy to affect the way they treated him. But I knew that it wasn't me who deserved the thanks. When I was a bit older, I read this in the Bible – it's from Ezekiel chapter 36 verse 26:

> I will give you a new heart and put a new spirit in you; I will remove from you your heart of stone and give you a heart of flesh. And I will put my Spirit in you and move you to follow my decrees and be careful to keep my laws.

Here Ezekiel anticipates what Jesus does for his followers when he gives them his Spirit. He knows that the Spirit will change their hearts, giving them the desire to obey laws that would otherwise seem too hard to obey. Like the law that tells us not to covet what our neighbour has, even if they have just made it into the first team.

Lastly, the Spirit who actually *inspired* Ezekiel to write those amazing words, over 500 years before Jesus had even been born, is the same Spirit who lives in Christians today. 2 Peter chapter 1 verses 20 and 21, says this about the way that the Spirit was involved in the writing of Scripture:

> Above all, you must understand that no prophecy of Scripture came about by the prophet's own interpretation. For prophecy never had its origin in the will of man, but men spoke from God as they were carried along by the Holy Spirit.

So there is an additional way in which the Spirit changes the minds of believers: he enables them to understand the very words he has inspired.

No wonder the Bible is a closed book to many people.

Without the Holy Spirit, even great minds struggle to make sense of it. (And I thought that the Bible was best used as a source for unintentional references to rugby, remember.) But that is another way in which God provides for those who follow him. He sustains them through his word.

The Bible

C.S. Lewis, best known for writing *The Lion, the Witch and the Wardrobe*, emphasizes the importance of reading the Bible in his book *The Screwtape Letters* – an imaginary series of letters written by a senior devil to a junior devil. Their aim is to cause a man who has just become a Christian to lose his new-found faith. The senior devil tells the junior devil to make sure that the man's life is dictated by 'the streams of immediate sense experience'; in other words, *get him to rely on his feelings*. The devils know that when life gets hard for the man, he may *feel* that his faith isn't real. The solution proposed by the book – and by the Bible – is for the man to reassure himself of his relationship with God by focusing not on feelings, but on the *unchangeable promises God makes in Scripture*.

The truths contained in the Bible are unchanged by our moods or our circumstances. No matter how followers of Christ *feel* when they face opposition, they can look to the Bible and be reminded of what they know to be true. I don't know if you're a sports fan (you've done a good job getting this far if you're not), but think about how you feel when you watch your favourite team on TV. If you're watching a recording, and you already know the final score, your emotions are very different from those you feel if you're watching a game live. So when, for instance, the Bible tells us in Romans chapter 14 verse 11 that one day *everyone* will acknowledge Christ as Lord, even his fiercest opponents, it makes all the difference. It means that even if the opposition seem to be winning, Christians can be sure of the ultimate outcome. As Jesus says to his disciples in Mark chapter 13 verse 23: 'I have told you everything ahead of time.' Having the Bible is like already knowing the final score.

Christians (and the churches they attend) should take the Scriptures very seriously indeed. If Jesus did so, then his followers should certainly do likewise – especially given that they will face persecution just as he did. Jesus emphasized that knowing what the Bible says is the only way we can be sure our thinking is correct: 'Are you not in error because you do not know the Scriptures or the power of God?'[2]

Jesus, with all his power, authority and insight, certainly treated Scripture as the very words of God. (In Mark chapter 7, for example, he explicitly refers to Scripture as 'the word of God'.) Jesus lived, of course, in the time 'between the testaments': what we call the Old Testament was already in use, but the New Testament had yet to be written. Nevertheless Jesus anticipated the writing of the New Testament, preparing for it by choosing, appointing and equipping twelve 'apostles'. They were men who had unparalleled access to Jesus and his teaching, and their authority is such that Jesus said of them, 'He who listens to you listens to me; he who rejects you rejects me.'[3] The New Testament is made up entirely of documents written by these apostles or by those under the immediate direction of the apostles – the only

[2] Mark chapter 12 verse 24   [3] Luke chapter 10 verse 16

exceptions being James and Jude, who were Jesus' own brothers. In addition, Jesus tells the apostles in John chapter 14 verse 26 that they will be well equipped to record his words with accuracy: 'But the Counsellor, the Holy Spirit, whom the Father will send in my name, will teach you all things and will remind you of everything I have said to you.' So Jesus' endorsement of what we call the Bible is impressive.

Perhaps we shouldn't be surprised. 2 Timothy chapter 3 verse 16 says this: 'All Scripture is God-breathed'. Although 100 per cent of the book we call the Bible was written down by human beings, every word was the product of God's inspiration.

In a *Times* article, Stephen Fry once sang the praises of the Bible, with its beguiling styles and stories. It's true, of course – the form and content of the Bible are beautiful. But T.S. Eliot, perhaps the most important writer of the twentieth century, didn't agree with this view of the Bible as simply a collection of great writing: 'Those who talk of the Bible as a "monument of English prose" are merely admiring it as a monument over the grave of Christianity.' There will always be people who see the Bible in the same way that they see butterflies in a glass case: beautiful and dead. But, as Jesus says in John chapter 7 verse 17, 'If anyone chooses to do God's will, he will find out whether my teaching comes from God.' In other words, the proof of the pudding is in the eating: when we obey God's words, we see God's power working miraculously in our own lives. There's nothing dead about it.

My aim in writing this book has simply been to make people better acquainted with who Jesus is. But to be honest, there's no better way of becoming acquainted with

Jesus than by reading the Bible. As Jesus himself says in John chapter 5 verse 39, 'These are the Scriptures that testify about me.'

If you have questions or would like to find out if there's a Christianity Explored course running near you, e-mail questions@christianityexplored.org or visit www.christianityexplored.org

Acknowledgements

For a short book, Christianity Explored took a surprisingly long time to finish. Over the course of nearly four years, it passed through any number of drafts, revisions and rethinks. Our grateful thanks go to all those who have read these various manuscripts, offering suggestions, criticism and encouragement. We want to acknowledge the significant contributions made by Ollie Balch, Tom Bible, Dr Andrea Clarke, Paul Clarke, Jon Daniel, Ed Dickenson, Sophie Peace, Naomi Rosenberg and Edwina Thompson. In particular, the patience, dedication and intelligence of Sam Shammas have immeasurably enhanced each chapter. Lastly, our thanks to Tara Smith, who has been an astute and sensitive editor.

There is something in this book to offend everyone. Some of it offends us, and we wrote it. But none of the people named above should be held responsible.

Rico Tice and Barry Cooper
New Year 2002